The Corporeal Construct

Established October 2024 – October 2025
New York, NY
United States of America
© 2026 Baruch Menache
Published by McWest & Associates
All rights reserved. ISBN: 978-1-971928-00-5

The Corporeal Construct

Corporation, Performance and the Architecture of Social Reality

Baruch Menache

Contents:

PART ONE: PRODUCTION AND PERFORMANCE

The Architecture of Work

Production: Sequence, Labor, and Material Ends

We must distinguish from the outset that the corporation differs from the tedious work of physical duty which is ongoing for the sake of production. We can dismiss artistic endeavors which utilize the notion of production and physical duty for the outcome of performance. The tedious duty is following its innate productive end, while the corporate arrangement aims for performance alone.

Production is a sequence of movements which all can be defined as miniscule productions, where every sub-duty is producing a product on the chain reaction of final production. When we produce an agricultural item, each event in that process is to further the productive end. When there is an action of harvest, it is the removal of the agricultural item in whatever fashion to succeed to its able end of sustenance.

The act is to move in a direction that will detach the product from its origin. There is no deviation of that act as long as we are on the production sequence of agricultural products. How the act is done, or its performance level, will not deter the production of the act. The act does not exemplify itself and rather has the exemplification of a production outcome, which if not engineered would have all preceding acts to be superfluous. Therefore, even with a change in the manner or distance from individual to production, the exemplification is still the same: changing physical states for the purpose of a production end. This will invariably be that relatable aspect of an operational body to manipulate the physical realm for the sake of that change, irrespective of the body or subjective experience that it originates.

Each of those movements has only the objective of moving along a sequence to a final production outcome. Whenever there is deviation from that objective, the production seems to falter. Therefore, we can mostly associate production with physical activity even as the physicality can be removed to a certain degree. Whatever movements are reserved to balance the management of production cannot deviate from the production end and must perceive the enterprise as a physical activity of productive change.

This is why the criteria of production even under a system of management will become aligned with physicality and cannot represent any further element for society. The communal enterprise of production does engender a representation of a communal embodiment, but only for the sake of change for physicality which is its outcome. Thus, we can surmise that a production enterprise does not need the association with civilization and would produce just the same in any given context or environment.

The elements needed for a society of production are able body individuals who use simplistic comprehension to change their environment. There may be a communion towards that objective but this will be the only conceptual necessity. The difference between the agricultural process and the communal production enterprise is that it is reliant on a distribution of consciousness to culminate in that production.

From the vantage of the production process there is no difference. Once the conscious design has been ordained and implemented into the production system, there is only a conglomerate of actions that are for a production end. The representation will be the same as the agricultural process in that the organism shall enact themselves into a change for a production objective. The objective and the origin of that conscious design does not ascend in the sequence of that production. The ultimate objective cannot be attended for it would unveil the conscious design and depart from the notion of pure physical states of change.

To not deter the production enterprise from its application in the growth of consciousness and society there are two primary dynamisms that are direct derivatives: one, is the representation of the conscious substance which they service, becoming embodied in the production outcome; and second, within the enterprise there is a distribution of the conscious substance in spite of the awareness of its penetration. Even as a menial task is produced, one cannot help to recognize the conscious input that subsides in this action of a change of physicality.

In a sense, a partiality of the conscious substance is embodied and exposed to the producer in a more vitalized manner than could be impacted from either the drivers of the conscious substance or the partakers of the production outcome. There is the situation where the embodied instance can be explored at any interval, however, the usual case would have the producer who is embodying the activity to realize the potency and intimacy of a portion of the conscious substance.

The agricultural worker during a harvest will embody the design process that has led to the production sequence and its final outcome. They will always know something very intuitive about its elements, although, the intuition will not be realized unless prompted into conscious deliberation. The very act of production dissuades the individual from prompting that intuition for the task at hand demands the attention to the physicality of the sequence. The deliberation can only occur after the production activity. There is also a caveat to unearthing the intuition; there is a lack of context to purport a comprehension unless there is an overall exploration of the consciousness realm to which they must leave the production process. The intuition will still impress their personhood and can be extracted by the able conscious individual.

We can understand the historically measured process for evolving the production enterprise receivable to this very dichotomy of an impressed intuition that remains unextracted. Either the reluctance of the producer to follow that intuition or of able conscious individuals who do not extract the intuitive material to be applied to the conscious sequence. The production enterprise is heavily reliant on its internal system to evolve, which would necessitate the constituents to engender their exposure which will create a secondary conscious environment that could be re-inputted to the conscious substance for invigoration or be internally applied to supply the production that will espouse not only the physicality of the production but the underlying conscious sentiment and production objective.

However, another situation could be had, where there is an able conscious individual who extracts the emergent intuition that is exemplary of the production process and identifies a conscious structure that would sequence this process with less metabolic energy per production rate, which in turn hightails the production process.

We may assume the contrary, that the able conscious individual surveys a manner to further the production rate. However, one must first notice the individuation of the production chain and the intuitive response upon their component in the process. By determining a change in that individuation based on a thorough comprehension of their subjective material, the entire process can be changed. The assembly-line for instance is an understanding of the sociality between individuals in their respective production ends, allowing the merge of the social element that already was emergent in each individual. Upon understanding the sensibility of seclusion from the production outcome, it was understood that the constituent experiences a lack of connection between their task and the one that proceeds or succeeds it. They do not gain an exposure to the conscious substance as would a sociality of such a process.

Once the assembly-line was enacted, sociality allowed for every constituent on the production sequence to gain exposure to the entirety of the conscious substance. We may presume that this was not the state of affairs, and rather the able individual solely took notice of production rates and thus arrived at the conclusion of sociality for that objective. Anyone that has engaged in a production enterprise, even the production of the familybody, would notice that any attempt at precluding with attention to the production rate would not conclude to an ascendency of that rate. The entire production is dependent on the constituent factors which retain the material that leads to that production rate. Without taking notice of those factors and the material they embody, the rate will not improve.

There is another process that could alter the rate of production without taking notice of the constituents' material. To be precise, the enterprise is still noticing the constituents' material albeit the material that serves the sole purpose of action and devoid of metabolic and social process that accompanies it.

Henceforth, the primary factor of a change of physicality will be treated as the sole heir of the production process. However, when we remove the social and metabolic aspect to production it is a major deprivation of the overall process. Firstly, if there is no social aspect and the entire production sequence endures without a conscious exposure to its process or experience. The feedback from non-social forms are not in reference to the conscious exposure but rather to its efficiency in that production. Even if there were non-social forms that would mirror a certain conscious exposure, it would not be any different than a form that is external to the production process from conjecturing that premise.

The subjective social form will be able to experience the social eminence from the conscious substance and conjecture intuitive material. We have mentioned the primary reasons for such material; its extraction towards both the conscious substance and the production outcome. The non-social form that produces the outcome does not input a conscious substance on the production outcome, nor reinvigorate the conscious designer for adaptation and modification. The final product will retain those negative attributes, one, the sentimental disfiguration of the origin of the conscious substance which has not the experience of any able social forms to relay a true experience of the production.

Secondly, the product will be recognized for its missing social form in its production process. These are the attributes of a social form who receives a certain conscious substance, retains some of their own, and follows such partiality in the production sequence to apply a very subtle input. Of course, when the production chain is supplied with multitudes of social forms, those subtle inputs will amount to a product that wholly differentiates the other.

Production and Performance as Distinct Ends

There are two purposes for work in respect of the psyche and would mirror well with market demand. The first is to provide a separating haven between two reality states, where the work serves to avoid reality but does enough to be a contingent of reality that it provides that haven without the adverse effect of appearing to go against reality. The purpose of such for the psyche is the separation of consciousness because it can be taxing to be in constant commotion of its movement and needs. If there was a haven that disengages from consciousness but does enough to stay afloat with the determination to participate at some level with consciousness, then it proves worthwhile.

We often may think of this premise as arbitrary because it appears as an escape of reality, where it is not the optimal manner of approach to dealing with reality. However, the ability of engaging with consciousness is very much aligned with the availability outside of it, and with constant interaction it would be experienced at the expense of spatial interaction. This space that becomes available, even at the notion of being an escape, allows individual freedom to partake in a locale that does not continuously serve as a consequence of consciousness.

This purpose alone does not have the inclusion of any work that is constituted with biological circumstance, such as industry, but only with conceptual work, for it is an objective for the conceptual landscape. Any work that is truly considered work will not separate or distinguish reality from that domain, for the individual participates in a manner that is not conceptual, which then cannot offer a conceptual separation. For all work that is not conceptual will demand a consciousness stimulation, and one cannot conceptually separate when they are engaging in such work, for the mind will follow its biological movement.

Therefore, only a break from the industry would produce the ability of conceptual separation from reality, and especially this form of reality that manifests in work, yet would require a certain activity that would invoke a conceptual separation, similar to the conceptual work which utilizes that premise.

The second purpose is to inform upon reality from a vantage point that does not constitute itself as a reality. This, as well, would not be considered by industry standards to be work because a domain cannot inform if it is not separated from the domain which it seeks to inform. Therefore, industrial forms of work do not provide any intellectual material that can be invoked for reality, for reality itself is a participant of the engagement. Learning can incur, but it would be based on the specific dynamic reality and not in regard to anything other than the trajectory of the immediate concern.

Corporeal work, or conceptual work, will be a domain that would prove to inform upon reality by being separate from it but in proximity, making it somewhat relevant. This is where the difference of the constitution of the corporation will come into play; for if it were a habitat that is separate enough to be an inference, or too near to be somewhat redundant.

For example, banking is very near to market exchange, which will be problematic as an inference unless one develops its details in a manner that would provide such. While finance would separate itself to create its unique reality so that it proves to inform upon reality by its approximation. We can find that if it is too separate from reality, for instance academia, which finds itself so distant from reality that it loses its ability to inform but gains the advantage of being secluded and distinct from reality which does produce a high volume of learning that would not be available in the dealings with consciousness and its specificity. While academia will not be a great inference to reality, it will be offset by its ability to provide a database of potential inferences, which, if there is a method which leads to application, then it will prove very informative. While finance would be a constant inference, it does lack the separation that would maintain a development of the inferential properties and sometimes becomes lost with the market trend.

Bureaucratic and political institutions are near proximity to reality so that it will have difficulty inferring whatsoever; however, when there is the eventual inference, it is received by at the immediate moment because of its nearness. It offsets its problem of developing despite reality by invoking reality immediately preceding an inference.

Performance and Representation

The corporation will vehemently contrast to become the corporeal representation and dynamically opposed to the production end, one which only represents the physical change; a very small portion of the corporeal representation. We find it rather perplexing that a corporation can have any association with the production aspect. From the standpoint of the corporation the dictate of their addendum is fairly distant of an interaction towards the production aspect. The reception of that addendum is solely reliant on the distribution through the production workforce. They may adhere to the dictate through the manner of how their productive end is concerned. The production in reference to the corporation is to mold a physical portrayal of the already designed process. There is nothing to add to that other than the ability or capability of producing that desired result.

The corporation would like to perceive the higher-life-form through the observation of a communal body. The foundation of the corporation is the primary substance, unique to its mainframe, becoming the center gravity alongside the representation which consists of accessing the corporeal representation. Taking the counsel, guidance, and direction from that primary principle, they can enhance the corporeal representation through particular attention to a certain aspect of that wholeness.

Therefore, there are two elements that are engendered in the corporation, one is the reception, manipulation, amalgamation of the primary substance and two, the wholesome corporeal representation. This is why all corporations will observe a similar pattern of function while each particular will contain nuanced deviations; not due to an attempted modification of corporate society but in accordance with their primary substance which has its possessive influence.

The entire construction of the corporation is rather a conceptualized portrayal of a physical reality as paralleled with all conceptual frameworks. It takes notice of the interplay in the entire production sequence and uses its representation for the effect of creating a social enterprise that simulates those processes for the advantage of a corporeal representation.

Not alone does it use the production process, but it does become the bedrock of its system. Although corporations may follow a representation of the corporeal structure in a wholesome manner, they cannot organize their social function and physical parameters with a certain model in the production sequence. Within a conceptual framework, the notion of gathering for the sole purpose of representing the corporeal entity would not acclimate to "doing." The particular aspect of producing allows for the social organization to retain its structure, imbuing to its members that the objective is one of production, not performance of a representation.

We cannot convince able-bodied individuals to partake in a social organization in which they endure a representation of a reality, but are in a simulation for the sole production of more simulating effects for society. That reality would not engender a populace to strive for a sentimental self-sacrifice of their physicality for the mere representative effects, although that is a basis of consciousness which they would acquire.

Therefore, the social structure is largely borrowed from the production process, imagining a sentimental physicality to be considered "work," even when no actual "work" is being done. We are so deeply embedded in this modulation that we equate the notion of work within the context of a corporation with that of a production enterprise, even though one is simulated while the other is real.

In a corporation the most physical manifestation of work we can imagine is the commitment to remain within that simulation rather than being in any other locale. We parallel the notion of commitment with work in order to have the simulation of work as more concrete. However, commitment is merely a regular theme within the psyche, which partitions its compartments for different locales and interactions. What we truly mean when we say we are committed to work is that we are allowing a partition of the psyche for a simulated locale, where the end result is a performance or representation.

More precisely, it is an acceptance of a simulation in place of reality for the sake of representation. This is quite analogous to the construction of a familybody, where there is an acceptance of simulation; not a true social experience, but one that offsets that premise with a definitive representation of the corporeal structure. We acknowledge that a familybody is a simulation because, prior to its inception, there existed a sociality that was not confined to specific individuals; now, however, the social sphere is limited to these specific individuals. If sociality is considered the breadth of society, then the familybody is surely its antithesis. Yet, the representation of the familybody is so enduring that we find it difficult to accept this premise.

We have opened up a further inquiry into the familybody and its coinciding membership to corporeal representation to thus find inadequacy with the corporation. However, the corporation differs from that of the familybody by its mainframe being that of production, or material change. The familybody is constructed from biological mirroring, and its language demonstrates that. The corporeal representation of the familybody is the biological aspects of personhood, which do not incorporate the social sphere or multidisciplinary conceptual themes. We could incorporate the familybody into the social sphere, a socialite familial entity, or through participation of conceptual comprehension through identity frameworks. However, this is not the primary basis or function of the familybody.

The corporation, on the other hand, represents the corporeal position from the vantage of production or its physicality, and therefore becomes the structural representation of the state. The corporation, under its duress of physical production, cannot become a habitat for the inclusion of biological representations through familial attachments. The familybody is siphoned off from the social sphere for an extreme sociality which always finds the communal sphere detestable. The entire premise is to privatize the enduring sociality of society, while the corporation is deliberately attentive to society for its performance end.

The objective is to have the performance embedded into the representations of society for the social use of its conceptual material which is embedded in representations. While it does not espouse to be a social center, it does associate heavily with the society from whence sociality is born. The recipient of the performance is not the individual as would a social system, but the entirety of society. Much like its production counterpart which has the objective as an object or service for society, not individuals. We arrive at another pillar of the corporation: performance for the advantage of society as a whole and not in its fractions.

This sequels an inversion, where the corporation begins to represent society, being as the entire enterprise is solely focused on the reception of society. The societal representation that accrues from the corporation is not wholesome as would their objective to perform to the wholeness of society. To delist a corporation as being a detriment to society is fairly discounting, while delineating its representation of society to be shouldered. We notice that corporate culture will mirror a representation of society but only after an extended disparity, almost as if they were informed the latest. This is because they do not seek to represent society but only become a representation for society owed to their performance of a representation.

We must notice that there are certain industrialized features to the corporation which seem to contradict this sentiment. When we detect industrialized representations with conceptual constructs, we acknowledge that maintenance of the enterprise is at a loss with corporeal absoluteness and rather will obtain language as if they were in a production system with physicality as its nucleus.

Language that becomes industrialized is using the corporeal representation that is customary but without the absolute concern with the corporeal entity which they are all amenable to. Instead, there is a deviation toward the production attitude all the while to include corporeal representations; differing from the production enterprise, which also uses corporeal representations because it must use language that can relate to the systems without seeming privatized. They need to be efficient in their work, and added corporeal language offers the advantage of universalizing the production process.

The production enterprise does not appear as deviating from their tenets of physical change and production unless it becomes a habitual. When there is an over usage of corporeal language within the industry, the workflow begins to be ineffective because the perspective is as an observer and not a producer. To maintain the observation point of view will cause each task to be a deviation from that, which does represent physicality and its tedious movements in the sequence of production.

The mix of the two from the vantage of the corporation becomes industrialized language, for industry does not eminently require vernacular for its potential and could produce in silence. Language in its ultimate potential is the representation of substance, which is a necessity for a corporation and one which does not function in silence. A corporation must use language which includes vernacular of the production sequence. It also relies on the production vernacular to formalize the organization, as it must model that physicality to be considered a tangible construct.

Therefore, it would be necessary to incorporate industry language even as this is not their core tenet. We find that overly used industry language denotes a corporation that does not represent the corporeal wholeness and functions for an objective of self-defined values.

Leadership and the Limits of Production

The pilot of the conscious substance can compensate for these negative attributes by commanding multiple junctures of the production process. They will enter into the production sequence according to their conscious designs, or will place conductors who are privy to both the conscious endeavor and comprehensiveness of the production process.

Firstly, this does not compensate for the second negative attribute of a final outcome without social form imprinted on its process. Such an attribute is only possible with able social forms that embody a stage in the production process. Secondly, the conductors who are privy to both realms do not retain mastery of either one. We cannot have them dictate an approachable conscious substance as would be from the origins, and still further they do not comprehend the production sequence from the standpoint of interactive activity. They understand, but without the embodiment of a production sequence and its varying material.

Instead, the decisions will be a presumed conscious substance alongside presumed production ends. There is no ability to have them either become more oriented with the conscious substance nor with the production sequence, for they will cancel each other out. Had they returned to the production sequence then we would have reemerged with a social form that partakes in the process; alternatively, had they applied themselves to the conscious substance, they will begin to depart from the physicality of each stage in the production process.

Either the product of a non-social form production is consistent with these two negative attributes, or we have the driver of the conscious substance becoming more embedded in the production process to ensure that it delivers the proper production. When entering the production process they will either become embodied in the production which reverts the adverse effects or more likely, runs a synopsis that does not arrange for the various junctures of the production process.

When the latter is in effect, the product will retain one negative attribute, of an able social form to input the minuscule conscious applications. The same ruling applies to high-life-forms that are reduced to their capacity of physical change in which the social aspect is removed from the occasion.

Industry and Self-Sustaining Sociality

Industry facilitates the social layer that would not be provisioned had it not become a sequestered version of its process. By that very ability, it requires an indirect access to sociality, through which that animation allows to be representatives of that formidable layer. When the performance of industry does not have a parallel universe in the realm of existing sociality of a certain degree, then it performs as an industry to its version of sociality.

An example of this would be a complex and traditional university, being that it relies on a very expansive tradition that comes before it, and added to the complexity with which it deals with its present, it owes to a realm that is not institutionalized for a layer of sociality that is found beyond its doorways but, in effect, creates or generates its unique sociality. Although there is a found justification of its parallels in regular sociality, because it is not found but only justified, it is determined as self-sustaining sociality.

The ability to know the difference would be if we were to take away the institution: would there be a noticeable shift in the procedure of sociality? We must remember that even if there is an effect, and that may be the very reason to sustain a self-sustaining sociality, an effect does not transpire to be an existing layer.

Industriousness and Its Social Consequences

The term "industrious" is commonly defined in academic terms as someone who is diligent, hardworking, and consistently engaged in productive activity. It implies perseverance, efficiency, and dedication to completing tasks, often with a strong work ethic. In economic and social contexts, industriousness is linked to productivity and the ability to sustain repetitive or demanding work over time.

However, when we examine the term more closely, we see that industriousness is not necessarily about perfect or creative work. Rather, it refers to systematic labor that lacks innovation or creativity. Industriousness involves executing predefined tasks rather than generating new, groundbreaking solutions. The focus is on efficiency, following set patterns rather than being driven by innovation. This suggests that industriousness is more about structured effort than creative work.

Industry itself is demarcated as distinct, with each sector playing a specific role in the broader infrastructure of an environment. Industries are defined by their separation into specialized sectors, allowing for structured production and categorization. In this sense, industriousness is aligned with reproducing products from raw material, but without focusing on the raw material itself or the end result of those products. The person being industrious follows a set process and is concerned with execution, not the broader implications of their work. This means that industriousness focuses more on process continuity than on understanding the origins or outcomes of that process.

An industrious person, therefore, operates in a system where the task is to continuously repeat a predefined pattern without concern for the quality or end product. The nature of industry and industriousness emphasizes repetition, which inherently limits attention to the quality or details of the products or tasks. This is why an industrious person cannot focus on quality in the same moment as they are focusing on repeating the task. In this repetitive process, the focus shifts away from the specifics of the product itself, making quality control an external factor, not something driven by the individual's actions.

We could even venture to say that an industrious person, without an external quality control mechanism, can easily deviate into activity that is socially disruptive. For if one is required to perform a repetitive task at an optimal level, they would need to remove any obstacle, whether it be other systems, groups, laws, or individuals. The more focus on industry would give less perspective on the value of those deterrents and the ease with which they are disregarded in the process. It is not a problem of the personality of industriousness but rather the lack of quality control, which must be acquired outside of the individual's perspective, usually from a social group or intimate partners.

This dynamic contrasts with sectors like agriculture, where the producers' direct involvement with raw materials is inherently connected to quality. Quality is the namesake of the trade. If the farmer produces bad quality, it is perceived within the direct trade itself and not as a result or outcome. In contrast, industries must separate production from quality, making quality control an essential external mechanism. This external quality control is necessary because industrial processes cannot focus on quality during the repetition of tasks. The lack of internal quality control in industry proves that industriousness, by definition, cannot be about ensuring quality.

Moreover, the distinction between industry and sectors like agriculture can also be seen in fields like finance. In the financial sector, some institutions, such as banks, operate like industries, focusing on the repetitive task of currency and interest. The end product, the customer or the source of liquidity, is not the focal point. The focus is on the efficient execution of transactions, not on adapting to broader market conditions. In contrast, other sectors of finance, like market analysis, are more dynamic and adaptable, considering the broader economic context, such as future trends and the source of funds. According to a study by *Merton and Bodie* (1995), financial institutions that focus on efficiency and repetitive tasks, such as banks, are often seen as operating within an industrial framework that separates production from end-use outcomes.[1]

This distinction between repetitive tasks and market adaptability also helps explain the high regulation of the banking sector. Banks are heavily regulated not because they present more risk, but because they lack the ability to control the full cycle of their transactions. Unlike sectors that have inherent quality control, banks require external oversight to ensure stability. Financial institutions play a critical role in controlling liquidity and credit flow and their stability impacts the entire economy. As a result, the financial sector's stability depends on regulatory oversight to ensure accountability, as they have no means to access the efficacy and ethics of what surrounds their systemic input. The broader financial system, which of market analysis, is fully embodied into the ethics because it encompasses the full spectrum of the system, providing a very different perspective.

---

[1] Merton, R. C., & Bodie, Z. 1995. A conceptual framework for analyzing the financial environment.

Because of the systemic nature of a system, like in the case of industry or the industrious person, it mirrors the infrastructure as it exemplifies in accordance with its most expressed matter. Obviously, there is a complex layer to every perspective upon infrastructure, and by that we mean the physical structure of civilization and society, but in the industrial standard, infrastructure is merely the most expressive aspect of what is perceived.

For example, an industrial mindset would view vehicles as the most generative of a society because they are the most expressive in their form; highly mechanized, complex, loud systems that intervene in daily life. This is not to say that vehicles are the most true in their nature of infrastructure, but rather that they are the most expressive and thus noticed the most, being attributed as the system itself.

The industrial mindset, for example, and especially in the geographical and cultural locations of industry, is usually separate from regular residential areas, unlike corporations, which are deeply embedded and market trends are almost in the same location as residency. This is because industry perceives the infrastructure as its raw physical nature, which is the task at hand: to repeat the process of the system itself and its eternal state. Within industry or the industrial mindset, this is perceived as the most civilized element, despite the fact that they are culturally and geographically separate. The very attribute that makes them geographically separate notes this complicit argument.

For the civilized arena, infrastructure is perceived as a more complex system, industry disrupts that by taking a reproductive and systemic approach. The justification for industry being geographically separate is usually placed upon markers such as estate value, land availability, and so on, even though the true reason for their separation is that their perspective does not highlight the full scope of the system; unlike the corporation, which embodies as much of that perspective as possible.

Part Two: The Corporeal Construct

Anatomy of the Corporal Construct

The corporal construct is one which animates itself according to its principles, and its fundamental principle is to articulate or exemplify sociality, whether as a whole or as social sentiment. It is the namesake of sociality; it becomes beholden to the cause of sociality and its permutations, since, as the holder of that namesake, it has no access to its preliminary data.

It would be wrong to consider it simply as the preeminence of corporal constructs, for it is more so the entire animation and procedure of the corporal process, and any other effects are other than the direct perception of sociality. There seems to be no other construct that is as dependent on sociality as the corporal process, since it doubles from itself, and by becoming, it must rely heavily on the original embodiment.

It can be the cause by which a corporal construct would succeed in discounting, discrediting, or disrupting the preliminary factoid that lies behind the movements of its constructs, such that it seeks to be free of its shackles in at least an attempt to control the preliminary sociality. This is done in order to continue its internal process without major movement. It is only normal for a corporal construct to behave in this manner, as it makes sense, it is to act as the human and, eventually, in the role of being human, to discount the actual human.

Whatever role one may take, in the very extension of their role and the awareness of its discrediting; to inhabit the role is to begin to take upon oneself an attempt to discredit the human endeavor upon which the role depends. The trajectory or proper direction of the corporeal construct reestablishes itself as the role that it performs and in the recognition that they are merely a namesake of sociality, to do so perfectly, but in the awareness that that duality exists and that its internal construct is without authentic reality. This is the reason that a corporeal construct continues to animate life both in breadth and scope; it articulates itself rather than disrupts the process, allowing for the entire procedure.

The problem then becomes when the namesake of "human" overtakes the sentimentality of the human; it proceeds to be the solution within itself, relying more heavily upon degenerate forms of human aspects which happen to be miscalculated and have become outsiders to corporal constructs.

In the event of corporal overhaul, all savory characters are tethered toward corporate procedures. The eventual outsider, who does not entangle with corporal process, may be among the most degenerate kind, for they notice societal process and thus become the beholders of civilization to be socially charged. For then, their entire sociality is reliant upon weakened forms, for all other forms are either incorporated into the corporal construct or discredited, such that what comes about is meager sociality; and thus the beginning stages of degenerate corporal procedure, for it is the re-articulation of diminished sociality.

There is a certain negative sentiment that arises from within a corporal construct with the subconscious realization that it has no effect on direct sociality, more so that it does not contain it, whereby it is realized as simply a showcase of sociality and thus without purpose other than a third-party perspective. A first-person overview of a corporal construct has no effect, whether on the person or the organization; it is only the third-party, upon which ultimately the individual can take the helm that has any purpose or reason for a corporal construct.

Although there is an element of distribution of conscious sentiment or sociality, such distribution is simply the automatic element of the corporal construct, but it is not, in effect, distributed. This is not the individual distribution, nor the details of distribution, but rather the namesake and surface of social elements that are rearticulated in the corporal format. Without the intellectual details of that corporal construct, it is a codex that has no individual access and thus does not partake in choice-making or resolution.

THE CORPOREAL OBJECTIVE

The corporeal purpose, and when neglected becomes noticed, is to provide a stability of reverberation from a vantage perspective that overlooks the corporeal representation. The only method for this to be accomplished is to depart the corporeal experience and enter a perspective upon the corporeal instance. This would mean a fair penalty of divergence of all first-person personhood, which would seem to be somehow worth the endeavor. Without the corporeal perspective, a continuous first-person narrative begins to become overbearing upon its own weight. The continual manner has one always obliged to follow the rather arbitrary circumstance of individuality, to which a web of biases and disruptions cause failure of being too centered.

The centric focus has one gain the feeling that they are at a loss to the continuum, where the ever-present system becomes oppressive by its means of regularity. Even as the first-person perspective is not an endeavor that seeks to uproot the wholesome experience, by the nature of being within that state, one becomes detached from the wholesome nature and begins to follow a very specific set of parameters that has been conjured by the mind against the good reason of a wholehearted system. With the notability of never having the opportunity of departure, all good tidings of that state begin to take the appearance of an overlord, with each new demand as further evidence.

The continuity does not have the ulterior motive of creating the demand, only that inability of separation creates such an experience. With that being the case, one will reconstruct the entire centric system to divert towards the ease that would allow them some repose. In this manner, one becomes a shadow of their former selves, for only because the maintenance of continuous development is one that has become oppressive.

We find similar parallels with those who participate in continuous rumination, in which, without a proper separation, one begins to follow a very distinctive version of it; one that only follows the most essential aspects while neglecting the wholesome encounter. They do this because the expense of resourcing a wholesome encounter begins to appear oppressive, as there is no methodology for departure from the system, and without relief, individuals will choose to avoid an experience that would inevitably lead to that. This is the same in many other arenas of life, where the lack of a possibility for departure leads one to reconstruct the current system to be as idle as possible so that they never require to reach into a state that has no resolve.

Another reason for the injunction is that one who is not centered in reality, where the psyche is a trillion-parameter system, will at any time be participating only in a partiality and in sometimes non-consequential experiences. With such a large and complex system, one will inevitably become lost unless there is a departure with an incurring perspective that considers the entire corporeal representation. This is why the disruption to the entire continuity of the psyche process is both good for its very sake of decomposition and for the perspective that is gained from the outside.

The first reason, experiencing the system without relief, would be resolved only if there were a distinct separation; and the second, one losing a centered base in the system would be fixed merely by disruption and thus an organic re-centering. Yet centered oppressiveness or disillusionment is not the only problem, and mere disruption of conscious continuity would not provide that feat. Instead, because disruption of conscious continuity still follows an internal system, it will retain strands of the prior inclusive membrane of the centered system. To put it another way, when the ego becomes disrupted, whatever follow-up circumstance emerges will be a remodeling of that very ego.

The only way to disrupt the ego in its entirety is to follow an external perspective with its volatile center, engaging a perspective upon the corporeal structure that has no lineage to the ego. One can place the ego into the space that is reserved for corporeal representation, and this would have them utilize the third-person perspective as a methodology to continue their centered theme of personhood. It seems strange to have one place their ego in a locale fully reserved for disembarking from centric personhood, for why would one enter such a locale when they can simply remain in first-person experience?

ENGINEERING THE CORPOREAL

Although the engineering of a corporeal construct is merely that of systematic sequencing, without the formal "human" component, that of relating, it is still a very powerful aspect if used in a certain manner. Not all systems can be reduced to their systemic parts, as though there is simply a mechanization of components; and this may be the reduction that causes one to assume the worst of a corporeal system, that it fails to be more than its parts.

Besides the evidential nature to the contrary, there is the lack of articulation of systems, and especially the corporeal construct, which allows for such reduction. As we have mentioned, the corporeal construct is the receptacle and re-articulation of sociality, and just that simple definition does not allow for that reductionist view. For if sociality is of a certain caliber, its re-articulation is the exemplified version of that, not the systems that make it possible, but the presentation and representation of such an aspect.

Of course, if we were to understand the engineering we would propose that reduction, as systems will always remain systems, but it is the manner of its purpose or the intentional direction of a corporeal construct that is the most significant component of its design. We do not concern ourselves with its engineer or with how it proceeds to endeavor that subjectification (as if it has a subjective view), but rather that it is the intentionality that allows for its service and participation in sociality. The matter of its exemplification can be so significant that all other socialities are reliant on it; and without its continuous presentation, it would cause the degenerate state of all the uptrend of sociality; for example, governance.

There is another component that is also determinate to the corporeal construct that is merely overlooked due to the focus on its engineering. This is the manner in which it is structurally ordained. Differing from merely its exemplification, there is a perceptual component in service to the structural environment, which would do much more than offer a social presentation of its intention. Being bound to infrastructure, it makes itself both a corporeal construct and part of the perceptual realm; and without the corporeal component, there would be no possibility of its structural component. Not only is it for the purpose of the perceptual realm, upon which sociality and all else are dependent, it makes possible the structural competence that would not exist on a social level.

The reason for this is the immense intersections that make up the corporeal construct, as well as its continuous re-articulation of many different premises of sociality, and finally the mishap of human input, which then proves to only add to that competence. With this perspective, the corporeal construct makes way for a level of competence that no social or group-social formation can ever perform, and it is this performance in the structural environment that finally serves the most perfected aspects of the perceptual realm.

Very few of the corporeal constructs reach this level of competence, and more importantly, this aspect of competence does not regale universal consciousness but merely a position in the perceptual realm that is worth inquiring about. For one, if a corporeal construct is not structurally positioned in a perceptual realm of consequence, or if general sociality does not partake at its structural setting, then it will not be of the competence we are discussing.

For the latter, it is without participation of general sociality at the point of structural position, and in that way all its proceedings do not direct inference in the perceptual realm. Thus, most corporeal constructs will not be afforded this premise, since they are avoidant of general sociality, especially as concerns the position of perceptual placement.

Secondly, even if such were allocated, the specific location is a very considerable determinant, since if the surrounding perceptual realm is underdeveloped or less than adequate, it will not participate in that inference; or worse, being in participation with the underdeveloped aspects of the perceptual realm, it may offer a detriment to that realm. This does not lead to a complete degeneration of the perceptual realm because the corporeal construct is still bound to sociality and as such will be controlled, both indirectly and directly; if it proves too much of a detriment to the structural realm; e.g., mafia.

The exemplification of the corporeal construct still exists despite the lack of structural positioning, as that is merely a byproduct of construction. There can be no intentionality for the corporeal construct as an offering to the perceptual realm, as that would involve the very few minds determining such allocation. This would eventually result in being limited with possibly another structural shadow for the environment. This is something that cannot be done from an intentional standpoint, but merely to allow the corporeal construct to perform itself and recognize the clauses of participation and perceptual location; the rest of its service will be done through its mechanized internality and unprepared human input.

This is also the case in corporeal constructs such as names, life themes, and universal aspects. In these as well, through structural positioning, there will be the same effect on the level of competence which cannot be intended. A person cannot pick a name to understand its structural positioning, like the name of a country or historical location in the enduring recognition of its finalized inferences, but the name will perform as a corporeal system that continuously builds as dynamism between itself and its existing landscape.

Modes of Corporeal Dissolution

A corporeal structure can diminish in one of three ways, and either can be contrasted to a broader structure to which it represents itself, or it can be existentially separated from the corporeal structure; nonetheless in naming its structure separate from the sequence, much like how this work approaches the corporeal structure. The manner of integration, where a corporeal structure continues onward to a broader sequence, is only through a conceptual dialogue, much like contrasting two sides of a point allowing for the perpetuation of the corporeal structure outside of its normal function, integrated into what is the newfound subject of inquiry; that of something broader than itself, whether such is another corporeal structure or general sociality.

In the case of general sociality, not only can the integration occur through conceptual bridging, but also through representation, which has the original corporeal structure represent itself in front of the newfound approach to general sociality, almost as if to provide a demonstration of what this corporeal structure exists as. In that case, the corporeal structure will diminish by its dynamism toward that performance, although the subjective state of the performance is lacking to a substantial degree as such a state is unapproachable to its experience, more so its expansion of mind or personhood.

The third approach to the disintegration of a corporeal structure is by existential separation, that is, to differentiate through a mental process more so than anything found in a physical parallel. It is to understand the corporeal structure as it were, as a standalone objective and subject, such as the idea of the entire appropriation of that corporeal structure. By definition of its understanding, it has the individual who is behind and beholden to the understanding become differentiated, that the naming of the corporeal structure itself automatically differentiates, as well as the more complicated process of posturing individuality and delineating the corporeal structure in lieu of that individuality. At the same token, it is to approach that differentiation as it were, whether by describing it or by its extreme mental separation.

Thus, we have three approaches to the dissemination of a corporeal structure. One is the integration through conceptual comparison and contrast, which is most lengthy of the three, because it requires a constant accession toward the subject. The second approach is representation of the proprietary corporeal structure within general sociality, but it may be attempted in another corporeal structure with less effect. We articulated this within that new corporeal structure as though it were of that process, with some lineage back to that initial corporeal structure, but having difficulty connecting to the vitality of the original corporeal structure without much due process.

In the case of representation within general sociality, it becomes more of an effect, such that one can find themselves becoming the emblem of the original representation, much like the name of general sociality or the name of an organization or other such aspiration. The third approach is to structure dissension of its prominence within the psyche, and it can be done through a psychic mechanism of separating it from individuality, or to articulate the corporeal structure to a point where it is noticed as a structure rather than the experiential habitat or process. This is why a generation of philosophers usually precedes a generation of corporeal strata, for they are the generation that articulates that original corporeal structure, whether in order to disseminate that corporeal haven or to articulate it for integration with further sociality.

Misuses of Corporeal Representation

We find that there is an amenity to have the ego participate in the corporeal representation because it has protection from its dismemberment. The corporeal representation does not postulate to revert any individual reality, as it has as its model the continual focus upon the wholeness of personhood, so that it does become a safe haven to placate the ego or the centric state without the undoing damage that will incur if one remained in first-person volatility. The corporeal representation has as its calling the respect of personhood, and when inlaid with a centric aspect, it will serve to fulfill that premise alongside all else.

The caveat to this sleight of hand is that the corporeal representation does provide an inclusive overview, so that even if we slipped the ego into its environment, it will not remain focused but rather upon the entire corporeal experience. Due to this, the corporeal representation will continuously disrupt the centric aspect of the ego, placating to resolve towards the entire corporeal experience.

This is why one who inputs the ego premise will reconfigure the corporeal representation to be a very strict standard of options, to which by its controlled environment of certain pathological theories, it will ensure that it protects the ego without overreaching to respect the entire corporeal picture. This usually manifests as a pathological assumption of sociality to which the corporeal representation is to prove a certain stature of individuality. In this reinterpretation, we have a third-perspective, that is to ensure individual stature rather than representation; and with the assumption of sociality to be on board with that premise, it becomes repackaged.

The reason one relies on sociality to reinvent the perspective is because without such societal backing, it would come to appear for what it is, a process to ensure one's stagnated center without the overall representation of the corporeal instance that would disrupt that. When we have a social body that is in agreement to that premise, then we can ensure that it is not an individualistic recreation but rather the true nature of corporeal representation; as if sociality has gathered to agree to instill the current ego to remain in stagnation without the ability of change.

We also become aware that there is usually a fair link from a recreation of the corporeal representation to biological necessities. This recreation requires the justification of its entire premise, in the usual case it would be for the aforementioned but in this case it is only to remain in stagnation. Therefore, the trades that are mostly invested in the biological benefit for selfhood would be its manifestation.

Concurrently, selfhood has a distinct gain of benefit that does not need to endure much market exchange and laboring; it is as if one has only reached into the pot of biological necessities. Even as the premise is not for the biological needs per se, by inverting the clause to be directly such, the psyche becomes convinced that one is not engaged in some process for its benefit but rather a divergence to reach into the pot.

One requires a clear indication of the benefit to all such divergence, and the only chosen circumstance is the fulfillment of biological necessities. The ego and the frozen state of individuality do not require such divergence, since stagnation is not the same as a departure or disruption. This becomes a pathological trade of the market because all societal circumstances are only to reach into that pot, not for the sake of biological necessities but for the justification of such.

There is an aspect of truth that such a premise relies: the corporeal representation does sacrifice first personhood for its representation. This renunciation is for the entire corporeal representation rather than the installation of a still ego state. Additionally, it is not to be looked upon as a renunciation, because it is a utility of the psyche to find a perspective that cannot be distributed by its internal system. When one utilizes the premise that the psyche now has the allotment to maintain the current stature upon this external system, they are then engaging in a complete renunciation.

One would not consider it a renunciation to be distracted, because all would acknowledge that such is not a complete disruption but rather a necessary path without much detriment. However, when the corporeal representation is utilized to provide a still state of individuality, then there is a true renunciation because the entire premise is not founded on the psyche's needs, but only a reassertion of a former ego state.

This is why we find the resentful character arise in those who follow this premise: even as they continue to reassert their ego state and accomplish their aim; they do so on the backs of their entire personhood, with the corporeal representation becoming a wholesale renunciation of selfhood. The ego itself does not seek a still version to be instilled for further maintenance, since the ego is merely a stand-in for the current landscape of the psyche, for which the next instance would require a newly formed ego and a representation of the system.

Instead of a corporeal representation becoming effective when it provides a third-party perspective upon the wholesome endeavor of personhood, already, it becomes a generality, superimposing a position of the entire enterprise as if it can be culminated as such. By this very generality, it becomes effective only when it maintains its ambiguity toward that perspective. When it becomes specific and particular, it loses its corporeal representation. This is not an external formation of an ego, in which it represents personhood in its culmination of parts, but rather represents personhood as if it were from an objective point of view, not to be centered within, but upon that instance.

That differentiation is fairly significant, for it demonstrates the corporeal body not for its particular contents of engagement, but rather for what it becomes of value in the market exchange. The value of market exchange is merely the metric to retain a representation of what an objective perspective of value would be upon the corporeal body. The particular individuals who are given more market value do not ascertain that there is significance to their objective value, but rather to their corporeal significance and the structure of overall corporeal representation. The individuals themselves are not ascertained with an objective value; instead, it is the notion of person that becomes actualized in a more profound manner within these particular individuals. At no time is it a downtrodden perspective on particular individuals; it is only the advertisement of corporeal value or representation, onto which all individuals participate. If certain individuals are unable to embody that perspective in a better manner, so be it, but it is not they who are the essentials of that perspective, only an assistance to offer credence to the perspective of the corporeal body. Anybody can engage in the corporeal representation to enable themselves into the effect of that representation and the respect that it deserves, and it is not a limited exchange based on that market value.

INFRASTRUCTURE VS. CORPOREAL

To perceive the environment through its sociality, it would benefit by being viewed as either infrastructure or corporeal. We must define them accurately such that there is awareness in how they interact as oppositional forces while being in tandem with each other. Infrastructure, by its prerequisite, has an existential ramification, while the corporeal structure will always be distanced from existential participation. This is a backhanded way to describe the corporeal structure because that is the final outcome; there is a history of many family bodies, yet take no part in a historical record. Only civilization, its public sphere, and its traditions form that record. Of course, these family bodies did participate to some degree, although they had no existential ramification; only a third-degree impact.

We can find many examples of corporeal environments that do not existentially participate but can affect the existential measure of the public sphere and, thus, the private reception of it. A family body can technically proceed without existential ramification. Therefore, it does not existentially *exist* except in reference to the public sphere, or in how it distributes the process, which is ultimately only in how it interacts with the public sphere.

Another way of distinguishing infrastructure from the corporeal structure is through its connection to the central locale, which is the center of infrastructure. Of course, we must agree on what constitutes a center, but we can be assured of a fair agreement through social study. Once we establish a center, we need only study the connections to it, in how those connections function.

Any locale can then be determined as either connected to infrastructure, thus an extension of it, or disconnected at some degree, making it a corporeal system. The distinction is transparent: that which is adequately attached to infrastructure is considered infrastructure, neither more nor less. That which extends beyond infrastructure is considered corporeal, and that which is less than infrastructure is its shadow; such as a small house on a highway.

A third way of understanding infrastructure is its distance from political infusion. When infrastructure receives a degree of political sentiment, control, or regulation, it becomes corporeal. However, the absence of political influence does not necessarily mean it is infrastructure; it only means it is available to infrastructure. A desert or an unclaimed planet, for example, is outside political influence but is not infrastructure. The inverse, however, is true: where there is high political activity, there is no availability for infrastructure, as political institutions do not manifest from the ground up as provisions of infrastructure. Instead, they serve as guardrails for infrastructure according to its primary objectives.

Political representation remains within infrastructure but does not directly affect it, as it is a representation of itself rather than an active force. The activity itself is silenced, and only the representation remains in public view. This does not directly affect the public but rather represents policing for the public, which becomes sufficient. Every constituent within that locality conforms to that representation and avoids deviation from the law. This manifests most aggressively when laws are in constant flux; when infrastructure determines which laws to protect and which to neglect in adherence to its representation.

A case study: Officers were occupied with apprehending a thief at a pop-up seller's table. When informed of an individual behaving recklessly in public, they dismissed it, stating they were preoccupied. The law, in this instance, prioritized theft from the pop-up stand because that is what the public demanded, whereas the other issue was not seen as urgent. Even though the stand itself may disrupt infrastructure, through taxation, real estate concerns, walking space, and more, social acceptance determined that protecting such was the officers' priority. In a locality outside of infrastructure, policing is always dictated by the officers' immediate preoccupation, as there is no defined direction from which to interpret the law. Therefore, in this case study, we do not find the officers as outside of infrastructure but rather as standing in for the sentiment of infrastructure, fulfilling its representation.

CONSTITUTION AND ROLE-PERFORMANCE

As we have noted before, there is a primary element of the corporation that distinguishes, secludes, and protects its environmental space from breaching, as a true form of sociality, and thus becomes disconnected from infrastructure itself.

Infrastructure, in this case, is all that leads from any sort of conscious association without disruption from an unnatural source. What is at the core of a formal hierarchy of consciousness that is distributed without limitations? The reason it ignores dynamic sociality, coinciding with direct interaction to infrastructure is because it does not want to participate in that realm, all the while following its own construct from the ground up. Its first modality is neglect, thereby procuring a hollow space, to which it is secured of a formalization of the system by way of a conceptual format, most notably led by its constitution.

We may need to say that the entire process of its elements is to perform in a hollow space that is both surrounded by infrastructure and regular society, but ignorant of its direct interaction.

The conceptual format is the only means of appropriation, because without consciousness per se, does this modality still work as a procedure? Conceptual frameworks are merely the intellectual process which allow for any attenuation, so that it does not adhere to consciousness per se, or infrastructure, for it processes that by its modality as the coordinator of perception; it is that which has allowed accession of consciousness, or the access, depending on the debate of its origin.

We have discussed before that the reason it must be a hollow ground, though it does have some criteria related to outside infrastructure and general sociality, is because it gains its vitality in a suboptimal process through such direction. Although it cannot be direct, it must be convoluted and distant from general experience within that domain. It must stand upon it but not realize its own vitality is provided by what's external to it; because it wants to act on its own but has no ability to do so. It is not a criterion that can access the required vitality necessary to keep such an organization afloat and permeable as an experience within a spectrum.

Within such an organization, the sociality is constructed in a numerical format: the members exemplify themselves according to its structure alongside the inhabitants' state and their performance in that regard. They are inhabiting part of the structure, as if the individual has now become a seamless screw to an engine; thereby providing not sociality at an individualistic level, but sociality through the performance of that role and its subsequent dynamic with other roles which perform in an organized fashion.

This form of sociality is anything but real or genuine, so it does not necessarily have any reflection upon the broader spectrum of the individual or of infrastructure as a whole, but instead operates for the performance of the organization within itself. Each member of that sociality will constitute a brand that styles them, giving the appearance like furniture in a house, where other pieces of furniture interact with each other. Yet they are still inanimate objects and as such are not individualistic, but are performing in a manner that cannot be denied. The breakfront interacts with the dining table, and we speak in those terms as if they do interact, because in fact there is a form of interaction if we remove the notion of animation from the picture.

Without consciousness as a criterion for understanding things, we could say that the dining table interacts with the breakfront, because animation and inanimation have no concern for our interest, thereby allowing us to enter into the individualized space of objects interacting by virtue of them being an embodiment of the household structure. The organizational structure, or the constitution that sets in stone what particular roles can be inhabited in the first place, is the general criterion for whatever arrives after the fact. If an organization is concerned with creativity as a part of its structure, then roles will be inhabited by creative minds to take such space and produce a further spectrum of creativity.

Therefore, the roles are vastly limited according to the constitutional structure of the organization. In the example of the household, we specifically mentioned the breakfront and dining table because those are constituent roles for a household. But we did not mention a stapler or a stack of paper, for they are not part of the constitution of a household and therefore will not inhabit a role to interact with the rest of the household. If we place a stack of paper on the table, we would not assume an interaction between that and the dining table because the constitution of the household does not bear a necessary requisite for the correlation between a stack of paper and its constitution.

However, that could always be amended, and thus the household can in fact include the role of that stack of paper. That is when we discuss the interaction between sociality in a corporal structure: we are merely referring to having the roles interact in a fashion that allows for the organizational structure, based on a constitution, to follow its procedure to its intended effect. There is no formalization of interaction based on individuals and their criteria according to their needs as a person, for that has nothing to do with the organizational structure and thus is a sociality that goes against the general procedure of the corporal entity.

When a corporal entity becomes political, it is merely in the sense of its sociality applying a humanistic aspect based on regular infrastructure that has no bearing on the organizational structure, and thus threatens to cause the corporation to endure a direct interaction with its external mainframe. It is not political in the sense of necessarily bearing political content in a general manner, but rather political in the sense that it is now circling around material that has no agreement in the organizational structure, its constitution, or its varying degrees of roles that interact with its subparts.

It has taken the benchmark of access within the corporal structure to allocate for a humanistic aspect, or a non-organizational aspect, which is then assumed to take a role. It finally becomes political when there is a certain agreement in the organization to that intrusion, as if it is validated and accepted as a particle of the organization, when it is rather a wrong nail in a construction frame; accepted, but noticeably destructive to regular sociality, thus enabling others to engage with that realm of sociality.

For example, it would become political in a corporal entity to have some part of their sociality reach beyond the hierarchy of its organizational structure in order to obtain access that can only be agreed through humanistic endeavor; a relationship that is beyond the construct of the corporal system, to which all outlookers must proceed to interact with that subdivision of validating sociality. Thus, the organizational structure is split into that of roles to occupy based on the constitution, and roles to occupy based on this external sociality and the disenfranchisement of the hierarchy and its procedure.

When you have the opposite of such an effect, when there is no political orientation or threatening sociality that is humanistic, the indirect relationship on which the entire corporal entity rests has no way of accessing the conscious substance on the external front. As we noted before, the corporal entity must have an indirect relationship with external sociality and infrastructure, and thus requires some humanistic exchange that does not coincide with the corporal organization; much like an engine which only works if it participates in an assembly that makes the vehicle. In itself, the engine is an arbitrary form of movement without reconciliation.

Although the organizational structure is coherent in its internal frame, it must contain an indirect relationship with what surrounds it so that it could be experienced with the vitality required to maintain a semblance of reality and experience of dynamism. For this to be introduced, it must enter at some point. If the internal structure is so beholden to the organizational theme, meaning it is completely corporeal without any deviation, there is no entrance-way for indirect sociality and/or infrastructure to make headway.

Take our prior example in which we discussed the breakfront interacting with the dining table: the interaction has vitality not only based on the constitution of the household, but also because it was furnished, assembled, and designed in a realm outside of the household. This is subliminal and not part of the normal interaction between the breakfront and table, but is nevertheless necessary to participate in that sociality.

If we could somehow construct a breakfront and dining table in a manner that excludes external sociality, which would be fairly difficult, it would lose its properties of dynamic participation in the constitution of the household, despite the constitution itself being sound and the organization proper.

In the other example of the engine, to take it to its extreme: we do not want the corporal entity to act like an engine because it is wanting to be permeable to the outside infrastructure. While the engine does not work well with any deviation from what is external to it, it must adhere to its performance and direct purpose through the nuts and bolts that make such a feat possible. However, if we follow the specific nuts and bolts, we will come to realize that although they do occupy a role as purposeful engineering in the organizational structure called an engine, there is an element of its predecessor. This is external to the engine and in its history of development, which, although can not be seen or understood, is still required. The engine does require some sort of lineage to fulfill its criteria in the current moment.

We cannot fully understand what it is about the nut or bolt and its preceding history that allows the current engine to proceed in kind, but conceptually, it must be required. While the engine is different from the corporal entity, conceptually they are the same, at least in our understanding, even if we do not contain evidence of such.

Sociality enters the corporal entity by various means, but most often it is through the individualistic members and their humanistic traits which permeate the experience of that corporal organization. Another means is the physical space, which, although separated by its construction, still connects to infrastructure through doorways that allow for access.

Disconnection of sociality can work in two ways: either the corporal entity can distinguish itself enough that the sociality extends beyond its mainframe and becomes almost corporeal across the entire human structure; so that in their experiences with tangible infrastructure and regular sociality, individuals imprint corporeal aspects onto broader society, which then returns and integrates back into the system.

PERSONABILITY IN THE POLITICAL FRAMEWORK

There are various frameworks which one is embedded, whether agreed upon or otherwise, and it is these frameworks that are possible to be engaged in either a personal manner or avoided without personability. We have discussed in other works that the universal notion requires personal engagement not so much to offer its persona but more so because without a personal criterion of embodiment, a theoretical framework is unsustained and rather remains abstract to the experiential state of the individual and thus to all its manifestations within the longevity of its framework, including its proper format of complexity. Amongst all frameworks, the most prevalent is the political framework, and without its personability, one will engage with the framework in a subconscious manner, for everything is layered with a political framework, or in an abstract reconfiguration of what constitutes a political framework, despite the prevalence of a different sequence in the embodied nature.

If engaged in a subconscious manner, without a reconfiguration of what constitutes a political framework, one will be dragged along by that framework with little attention to its sustainability or to personal criteria. In such a situation, if a political direction takes hold, it is merely followed without significant adaptation or alteration, leaving one at the mercy of powerful frameworks embedded in exponential processes, yet entirely without power over their fulfillment or orientation.

Alternatively, if one recalibrates a political framework not from personal experience, nor offered in its personability, one will create an abstract sensibility of that embodiment, even though it is neither truly personal to the individual nor genuinely experiential. This approach avoids the personability attached to the political framework while still calibrating it as a sequence that retains regulation or orientation. Yet the entire basis remains an abstract configuration, constructed according to what would constitute an embodied state, despite prevailing data that may be observed all around.

Besides the political framework, which is the uppermost of the spectrums, there is the secondary political framework, whether by state, by city, or other secondary tiers, to which, if offered personability, one will have access to its criteria; but if avoided or recreated, one will have lost attachment to its sequential nature.

PART THREE: THE CORPOREAL SHADOW: REPLICATION AND INDIVIDUALITY

Corporeal Replication and the Pathology of Adherence

Creating the conceptual shadow can be done through corporeal injunction, where there is a premise of the corporate process at the behest of the individual social parameter, to a point where it replicates itself as though it is in contrast to itself. Just as a parent, the raising aspects of their child will be amplifying the parameter of the child despite the very fact that the child is an exemplification of them, so too the corporeal structure is a remediation and replication of an individual parameter or intrinsic sociality, to which it is a mere copy. While its functional sense is purposeful, it is without the beholden nature of the individual.

In its extreme sense, the corporeal injunction exemplifies the individual to such an extent that it not only replicates that individuality as a process, but does so in contrast to individuality; as though the one problem with the entire corporate structure is the fact that there is an existing individual behind it. This is the same creation of the overextended parent, who, based on their purposeful agenda towards the child, makes way for the creation of their individuality as a deterrence; as though the child is good on its own and has become anchored in a negative manner to the parental body.

The reason this occurs is because the corporeal process is the re-exemplification of an individual bearing, and doubles as a replicating factor, specific to how the corporeal structure intersects with individuality. For example, in the industrial process, it exemplifies the mechanism of the individual as a system of parts that follow a sequence, for that is the intersection of the corporeal process in accordance with the individual. Is the individual systematic as though a form of industry? And might it be a complement to term one, "industries," as though they have accessed a part of their individuality that intersects with the industry's form of the corporeal structure?

Such a re-exemplification is of great consequence when it supersedes individual capacity to follow its process without direct input, and as such, the tractor is the exemplification of an individual in their farmer work. As the individual plows, so is the tractor created to plow and act as the individual, but as a re-exemplification that would allow continuity or replication of the individual. Thus, still, the terminology to the power of a vehicle is "horsepower," for in how many horses has it replicated, or to be precise, in how many people does each horse replicate? Yet, such was not the question of antiquity, for it was not noticed as much, since the multiple was fairly diminutive compared to six hundred horsepower.

The tractor is then the replication of a specific aspect of a single individual, replicated in the thousands, but still can be reduced back to the individual. The point of extreme to the corporeal structure is not its multiplicity, or the aspect of intersection, such as industries, dignified, controlled, generous, and other corporeal exemplifications, but the adherence of the original man that made way to that process of corporeal exemplification.

When the adherence is to the extreme, where the individual does not allow the corporeal structure its autonomy, but rather succeeds to continue to propensate the corporeal existence, then it does not exemplify the specific aspects of the individual, but rather becomes the exemplification of in what way the individual fails as a specimen; more so that this multiplicity is then engineered to propensate that very notion. Not only do we have a semi-autonomous corporeal existence that is based on the negative contrast of the individual, then in lieu of industries, is sterile in the way a mad scientist might view it: it generates a multiplicity of such, six hundred horsepower of that injunction.

The sterile intersection is rather the soft wording of the negative perspective of the individual being a contaminant; to which cleanliness is not to allow for a new ascendency but to remove whatever existence may be there.

This is how the parental body proceeds to become the shadow of the child: by the propensity of adhering to the child's ascendency, which so happens to be a corporeal structure, at least in the perspective of the parent, which instead of allowing the child or the corporeal representation to proceed in continuation of the individuality of the parent, it is expected to be as different than the problematic aspects of the parent. Or, in the perspective of the parent, it is to propensate that negative attribute, since that is the direct association of the purpose of such adherence to the child. The parent is viewing the child through that internal negative attribute, but more so to propensate their entire parenting process to the continuity of that negative attribute. And as such, the child will begin to follow that demand and become a corporeal replication that has as its sole purpose the continuity of that negative attribute pertaining to the parent that made for the continuing adherence of such parenting procedures.

The adherence is the cause of the negative injunction to the corporeal structure. This adherence is the pathological focus of continuity to its replication, for if the corporeal process is a replication, and one dedicates their existential system to that, then they are stating explicitly, "Rather focus on the replication, for the original is faulty," which transcribes to the corporal system as, "The fault of the original is the only aspect required for replication."

This transition seems like a stretch, for it is one thing to take a negative approach to the replication, but for the replication of the corporeal structure to assume that it must generate the faulty aspect may seem contrary to any supposition or termed engineering. However, we forget that the corporeal structure does not contain an internal logic and relies completely on its progenitor, as the tractor can sit in wait until an individual takes precedence.

Additionally, the corporeal understanding of its process does not participate in the entirety of the individual's logic but only its last sentiment, which in this case is the "fault of the original." It is then coded not from the vantage of the individual who sees the experience of replication, for the corporal structure does not 'know' that it must proceed as a replication; it is not self-aware of its part in the process. The only injunction for it to rely is the latest existential direction of the individual, which is the "fault of the original"; in this way, it will replicate the specifics of that fault.

We can contrast this to the corporal system; following negativity will still continue in its multiplicity as wholesome. For instance, justice pertaining to the justice system follows the negative aspects in the abhorrence of society, yet succeeds in completing its process without regaling the multiplicity of that sentiment. This is accomplished through various means, but for our discussion, we only need to know that it is not the negativity through which the corporal structure becomes a multiplicity of fault, but adherence alone. In the case of adherence, it is the disillusionment of the individual for the replication, where it is not a specific negativity but the entire direction of individual disillusionment, which can be seen as more than negative; as existential degeneration.

The negative aspects of anger or crime in the justice system are part of a general sequence of the individual or society: anger, for the concern of a stasis in which no injustice pertains; and crime, for the society that is without crime; such that embedded in the very negativity is the wholesome nature to which it is attributed. In this case, there is no embedded positivity, for the mere adherence to replication of selfhood is the disillusionment to every aspect of that individuality. There is no truth to the matter, where somehow within that corporal direction will find the proposition of the individual and its succession.

Despite the parental body seeming very concerned with the succession of their kin, because of the disillusionment that is made aware from their adherence to their replication, they contain no bearing of a succeeding aspect to their succession. Even the very concern of kin falls away, based on the realization that disillusionment does not allow for any individual sentiment, including the very thing that caused that disillusionment.

Corporal Internality

A corporal system that decentralizes itself from all sociality, whether direct in proportion to its social externality, or indirect in proportion to a substantiation from within itself based on its constituents emulating social material based on an externality, then it will prove itself to be a problematic circumstance. In the usual case, with such desynchronization, it would become beholden to interactivity, and thus become the interactive realm and its various benefits and advantages. However, in succeeding to continue as a corporal structure, devoid of the natural inclination of interactivity that should surmise such a setting of separation, one is beholden to a corporal entity that is disconnected from all sociality. This we would term corporal internality. It is internal more so than in any way to manifest a form of social material that is connected to externality. We might ask what animates such a realm if there is no internality other than its supposing itself as a corporal entity.

This would be the animation of the individual participants based on their biological habituation that acclimates towards the realm. This is fairly different from simple interactivity because it is not interacting with the realm or its constituents, but is the exemplification of the individual stature as represented in themselves which animates the process. Since there is no other animation, whether of interactivity, for it is remaining a corporeal structure, as well as sociality, for it is sequestered from such, the only remaining de facto reality is the individual strata of exemplification and their biological stature. This occurs as though they are exemplifying themselves in the sacrificial realm of offering animation based on their reception of selfhood.

Although this might seem like a simple third option in the animation of the corporeal structure, it is most catastrophic for it is not the exemplification of the individual as a biological stature to which now it is corporally supposing itself in whatever the process that is being engendered, but rather the destructuralization of the individual in order to facilitate the corporeal structure. That the corporeal structure is now animated as the degradation of whatever is defining the human character of that individual because the transfer of material is the separation of selfhood rather than the animation of selfhood. When it finally reaches the corporeal structure, it is animated based on the separation rather than on its congruent exemplification that is suppositive of itself in the beginning.

What all this translates to is a corporeal structure that is operating based on the alienation of the individual as defined by themselves or as defined in its human experience. And thus is the counterpoint and a vengeful structure against all that is beneficial to an individual and to the way they describe their humanity in its fundamental sense.

SCALABILITY AND LIMITS OF INTERNALITY

The corporeal system is now being animated with social material, which would be interactivity in the regular case but is simply the permeation of the experience of social material at its interactive base; relatable and in-charged by itself. However, in this case it is the manifestation of the social material in its fundamental sense. In this, we gain a picture of what the beginning stages of social material are, and it is the exemplification of the individual as a strata of experience and representation. One is exemplified in their individuality, in the wholesome nature of their persona, and their embeddedness within an identity system or overall structure.

The reason that such is social and not corporeal in the fundamental sense is because it is the beginning stage of experience itself, where one moves between the idea of selfhood and selfhood in a single take and does not require some sense of the idea of self to stand above the experience of self. It becomes corporeal, in that it structures itself away from that first supposition of the interchanging notion between the idea of self and the experience of self, which is now allowing exemplification of that entire process once again. Such that when one interacts with this corporeal internality, they are doing so for the beginning stages of their individuality.

We could find this most readily when we attempt to interact with constituents that participate in such realms, and they are seemingly very disruptive of their psychological happenstance. It is as though they do not gain a stance of semblance of all that they prioritize. They are losing their ability to become aware in any way of the representation of, and how they have effectuated, their individual psyche. And more and more, they are reliant upon the input of that corporeal internality to define their selfhood.

Now that there is a codependent propensity for the individual to continue to relate information of selfhood through this corporeal internality, rather than through other mediums, they are beginning a learning process of the foundations of evil. This is because the corporeal internality is exemplifying the shadow of the individual, or in how the individual decentralizes itself. If we define evil as that which decentralizes what is a paramount social material, then this individual is beginning to learn that very process and become the exemplification of such. We may wonder if one who has been habituated to the degradation of social material in the decentralized manner, to participate in any corporeal internality, would have the opposite effect; where the corporeal internality would begin to become the exemplification of what is good and founded from its relation to what is destructive.

Limits of Scalable Destruction

Although I am unsure if this plays out in a true psychological and structural manner, we do see a parallel of the lack of succession of an evil-minded objective in the scalability that is required to invoke detriment on a large scale. Because it is possible that in the entranceway of invoking those sentimentalities into the corporal internality, which is the base layer of the creation of scalable corporal destruction, it reverts itself and then begins to exemplify the contrast of that individual input. This is the founded nature of individuality and in what way such individuality would be in its betterment.

The reason that scalable corporal destruction is only available in the corporal internality is because, in the regular case, it has to behave in the manner of concurrent social material, and it is constantly contrasted with other social material that eventually contrasts with all social material that permeates all of reality. In any sort of connection, whether direct in its real-time manner or indirect in its belated interaction but still very direct to the social system, it is impossible to create a scalable version of destruction in the manner of a corporal representation; and it is only available as individual or group phenomena.

Even in the case, for example, of a creation of that destructive power through the corporal internality, it is only possible to invoke that very destructive power through another corporal internality in the immediate succession of a corporal process that behaves in likeness to other social material. It would only be deemed effective if all social systems are in some way concurrent with that process. Even in the case of a mistaken possibility, it is also based on that very social material, for the mistake is realized beforehand in its measure towards the possibility of such a mistake. Thus, a scalable destructive measure of the corporal entity is only possible, even in its mistaken attempt based on the agreed social material. That is, if it remains a corporal process, not an internality.

Yet, to maintain a corporal internality, one has to behave in the manner of the goodness in their exemplification as an individual, or as a social exemplification of such, where it is contrasted in the creation of its shadow, or its detachment, to create the entire corporal entity in those that animate for its destructive force. However, in the case of the onset of an individual who is already acclimated in such a shadow process or perspective, the corporal entity that is an internality will create in the betterment, a scalable proposition that would define itself in position to all that the individual is contrasted to, which is that of the benefit of social development.

It is only in the stage between these two processes, where if an individual is supposing in social development, to then be contrasted with the corporeal creation of its destructive path, all without the individual being completely reliant on that corporal entity for vitalization. They will be animated to suppose that very supposition, which now will be contrasted in the corporal internality for the benefit of social material. That is the latent stage between those two juxtapositions that create the possibility of scalable corporal destruction.

The motivations to enter a corporal internality can vary based on a scientific attempt, a political one, or a monetary one. But those reasons are completely arbitrary to the final creation of the corporal internality. For instance, all social material does not enter such a sphere, and it is sequestered from all that detail. Even the supposition from which it was originally engendered does not regale in such a realm. It simply follows the corporal internality based on the constituents that participate in that realm, and their suppositions of selfhood exemplified for that process. Even if the constituents are controlled and regulated in a very systematic manner, it is still going to exemplify in the shadow of their elements.

This works well in the gathering of constituents that are suboptimal or lacking moral sophistication, and the grunt of such experience would exemplify unexemplary aspects of individuality, which are then converted to the corporal internality as the opposite of such; for now they are detaching and thus developing their supposition. This can even be a creative process to develop in a scalable manner. The moral injunctions of individuals developed by gathering them in corporal internalities that will automatically exemplify the counterpoint, which eventually will become their learning curve and the experience of themselves.

We might think, look no further than a prison or any sequestered housing of a political nature, but all of these follow a regular corporal injunction, for they connect structurally, directly, and indirectly. It is only in the case in which there is a deep structural separation, a political isolation, and a social separation that we begin to enable the process of a corporal internality. It is also the case that one must sequester the interactivity within that realm, especially social manifestation, for if not, would just create that realm to be a corporal process that has a direct connection to sociality. There is only the case where there is little reason to exemplify social material that one has learned on the outside, or to continue in an interactive manner that would simply create the interactive embodied realm.

This is only the case where the corporal internality exemplifies the contrasts; that of a good stature who is opposite such. This is only when the individual has not completely become acclimated to learning from the shadow of their individuality, which is the betterment of themselves. For if they are completely embedded in the development of their moral structure, then the corporal internality will flip and become its counterpoint, the destructive scalable force of that detachment of goodness.

As a point of measure in this entire process, it is still incumbent upon an individual or group to rely more on continuous, direct social material, for that is the continuous opposition that generates for itself and for what is beyond it in accordance with the concurrent direction. Although the corporal internality can bestow some level of complexification that is unavailable in any other realm, those can be mitigated through other factions, whether through the interactive embodied realm or the indirect corporal representation. And if all those cannot be to its effect, then we need to suppose that it is not for the betterment of social continuity, and thus is a detriment in its beginning process.

Although we have outlined benefits and detriments of corporal internality, its opposition in its beginning stage is problematic to social material and is a betrayal of that social continuity. If the incentive is monetary, then it is a monetary betrayal. If it is political, then it is a political one. If it is scientific or academic, then it is an intellectual one. But in any of these arenas, it still betrays the natural process of each of those realms, for if the academic process cannot be engendered in any other manner other than the corporal internality, then one needs to re-suppose their alignment to that intellectual lineage to continue and allow for that tradition to remain unstained by this deep isolation.

In the case of the political realm, if one is not adept at a political stage of becoming of the counterpoint without the corporal internality, then one must accept the level at which they can be a participant. To betray the social realm in order to simplify a political realm is a contradiction of terms, because the political realm is a representation of what is social.

The arena of monetary benefit in which there is a divisive separation between social material for that benefit, will not finalize in the continuing nature of engendering sociality. This occurs even in the monetary return of such a corporeality; it will not be used in any other factor other than in re-animating that social separation, and then one must ask if there is any benefit to monetary gain without a social connection.

Most developments can be re-coordinated into an interactive embodied realm or into the indirect corporal injunction. For example, most medical institutions, as noted from the terminology, are institutionalized or at least at some level an interactive embodied realm, thus allowing for both the benefit of medical science to participate in the social realm as well as remaining interactive for the constituents who can then return that social material at a later date.

It is almost impressive that most medical institutions remain at some level institutionalized, and it is understood that social material does not enter its sphere, but that interactivity remains the most important aspect of its construction, and second to that, the medical input and the benefits of such.

Although one might want to construct the realm that exemplifies, as the first and primary supposition, that of medical science itself, in doing so, it will create isolation of that realm that has no bearing on interactivity or benefit to the social realm, and thus would become a corporal internality.

There is the case of academic science that requires sequestering, or that the notions participating within its realm are not socially agreeable and thus require sequestering; if it requires a structural separation or a psychological one, one must ask if there is a possibility of creating that very realm in the interactive embodied system. If the medical field has enabled what would be troubling at the outset of regular social processes to be enabled in the interactive realm, one can find the counterpoint in academia, and if such is not found, then it would mean that interactivity is not forthcoming and thus has no reason to remain a supposed interest. If there is no social connection, nor interactive representation or exemplification of such, then it has no reason for being pursued.

In the case of monetary matters, there is always a succession between the corporal internality and its original propositions that remain connected to the corporal system, because it must enter the marketplace at some point. It will not enter via the internal realm of that corporal internality, since it is sequestered at every level and has no market participation. One can only find the separation from the corporal system and how it entered into the corporal internality, and develop systems to remain in the corporal connection, whether direct, indirect, or as an interactive embodiment, such as an institution, and thus remain both monetarily successful as well as socially participating.

Renunciation and Conscious Transfer

Renunciation is a paramount importance of any conscious or corporeal system. For the consciousness system, it is the transfer of each strand of consciousness throughout the hierarchy of its permeation. For the corporeal system it is the ability for it to function as a reservoir of experience that is separate and distinct from regular conscious function.

The purposes are fairly different, for one it is to renounce in order to validate, and the other is in order to transfer. When transferring consciousness, we may assume that the priority is to allow and facilitate both sides of the transfer. For it seems that there is a great loss if no transfer is heard or no amicability to participate from the other side of the transfer, making it seem as if one is performing a disservice to their existence.

However, that is the point being made in that we're notified that there is the existential risk that there is no transfer and only that willingness will enable a proper formation. Because the individual must not perceive what is external or being received, but is primarily preoccupied with the function of whatever conscious layer they do retain, it would almost seem as if they would never know whether the transfer is taking effect or not; although there are verifiable signs. The ironic aspect about renunciation is that, with any transfer, it is possible to perceive such as a corporeal function toward the overall conscious system. When one agrees to the transfer of consciousness, they accept themselves as limited into a sanctuary of function, giving over encapsulation of consciousness that has been regulated and controlled.

Part Four: Memory and Corporeal Dynamics

Corporeal Continuity and Consciousness

The corporal construct is most vulnerable in the volatility of the conscious continuum, so that, in its degeneration, so too is the construct; and in its expansiveness, so too is the development of that permeation. It is the bookmark by which it does not become overly exposed, but remains dependent on consciousness.

Alternatively, it is this very trait that gives the corporal construct an advantage: it can continue unabated over time, and even across locations, so long as it participates in a developing conscious continuum. However, it does not have an innate ability to control its external exposure; unless it plays the dice in that regard. More often than not, it participates in its internal construct so that it may be of benefit to the confidence that a corporal construct requires: devotion.

Even at its best, as an internal mechanism for the corporal system, it is still just as dependent on external volatility. Therefore, it is not a recipe for disillusioning consciousness into more adaptability or internal development. In the case of a disrupted internal system, the corporal construct will become either overly exposed or insufficiently exposed. In such cases, despite the developing nature of external consciousness, or its degeneration, the internal mechanism will degenerate within itself.

This differs sporadically from the interactive domain, or the interactive construct, which is part and parcel of the consciousness spectrum and is, in itself, a participant in that continuum. It is not that it is unaffected by volatility, but rather that it may interact from a vantage point that creates an advantage from the disadvantage of general degeneration. Just as one can interact with the same source in a thousand and one ways, even a degenerate system can be viewed from a specific vantage point to create a benefit according to that context.

OVERSTIMULATED MEMORY STRUCTURES

Memory shares many similarities with the concept of an overstimulated corporal structure. In some sense, memory is the association and attachment to a conscious substance, but can also be corporally actualized. The reason for this is that memory is the manner in which one will access those parts of the psyche that have been formatted with alignment to that degree of consciousness. It is not memory itself that is the provision, but through memory one gains access to that awareness and thus activates the brain as if it were in the experience of consciousness itself.

Yet there will always remain a distance between the source as a memory and current conscious experience, so that when memory is utilized for consciousness, it remains a partialized interactive locale. This does not mean there is no availability for new conscious actualization, but only occurs at the behest of that memory source, combined with the new development. In the way a new marriage follows the exposure of the previous one, it is only added with a new formulation. At no time can the second marriage become a fully formed conscious experience because it already relies on the prior one for that effect.

Corporal actualization occurs such that, instead of emanating directly from the conscious substance itself, it subtexts that substance, overcharging the recent and current corporal structure. This process cannot occur when the conscious substance is not remembered in full spectrum.

When one element of the current corporal structure is engaged, it is unclear why and where the emanation of that representation arises, thus utilizing the memory source but not its full remembrance. The very act of disremembrance allows for that possibility. Without the full remembrance, one does not have access to its lineage or the conscious arena, yet there is enough access to experience stimulation from that source. This stimulation is mistakenly attributed to the current corporal structure, which becomes over-actualized beyond its natural capacity or capability.

What then occurs is that the current corporal structure envisions itself more than it truly is, extracting embodiment from the psyche that is divorced from structural reality. The entire psyche structure participates in this actualization, extracting compartments of the psyche that are only accessible to a more elaborate conscious source. These parts are recognized only because of that conscious source. However, this realization is limited to a psyche that lacks the adaptability to fully comprehend it. This understanding can only be granted by a misunderstanding of its true source.

The psyche acts in a similar manner, in that it can only actualize whatever corporeal structure it adheres to, beyond its measure and capability. This occurs because one forgets the lineage of such consciousness, leading them to assume the vitality as homegrown when, in fact, it is sourced from distinct prior conscious exposure.

In the same way that a diplomat experiences nuanced development in whatever locality they inhabit; development that is directly attributed to their conscious association with their country of origin even as it may appear as though this development is occurring within the diplomatic state itself.

On top of this, the psyche may access and remember the entire lineage of consciousness, but because it adheres to strict standards within its interactive locale or corporeal system, it disrupts the process. In effect, it acts as two personalities: one that retains the memory and lineage of that conscious source, and another that adheres to the strict parameters of the interactive locale, as if there were no other conscious source.

The Role of Structural Organization

We can parallel this structural organization, where there is a possibility of creating a structure with a certain attachment or association to a conscious substance, or more centrally, to the consciousness framework. However, because the elaboration of that structure overcompensates for the permeation, it extracts more than its allocated attachment.

In reality, no extraction beyond the amount of mutual permeation is possible; instead, it utilizes a small measure and recreates a version as if it were a high degree of consciousness, all due to its structural demand. This can only occur if it denies the lineage of that conscious system, acting as if it were a secluded, novel ground-up development, despite deriving all of its promise from its direct lineage to the conscious center or its various portals.

It must deny that lineage to create an elaborate corporal structure; greater than the normal dynamics of that lineage. Once that denial is in effect, there is no restriction for creating a corporal structure that draws from the conscious lineage it is connected to; recreating it at a higher depth, amplifying its elements so that it, in some sense, acts like a conscious center. However, its reality remains dependent on and subservient to the true center.

If one were to follow the current dynamics of the system, they would not be permitted to elaborate beyond its hollow entity. Due to the substitution between what is connected and what is its own creation, it borrows from thin air and exemplifies through imaginative proportions.

We can observe this in the amusement park. The amusement park does the same thing with association and connection to conscious substances as purposefully limited, yet elaborates in its corporal structure to a finite degree.

In this case, it does not deny the lineage but instead chooses specific terminology like "amusement," recognizing the entire structure as a self-conscious, fantastical realm. Because of this self-awareness, it does not act as a receptacle of conscious substance but as an interactive locale where promise exists in its attractions, not in its direct lineage to consciousness. This is only possible when one separates and bounds the entity (the amusement park or system) from conscious permeation.

Contrasting the Inner Psyche

We can contrast this with the inner workings of the psyche. One can recognize that the locality which they are participating in is distinct from its connection to consciousness. Whatever attraction and association it does contain are tangible and available for interpretation.

In this way, it is treated as an interactive locale, despite its exemplification as something else. It becomes separate from the conscious lineage and acts as a simple interactive space, much like a family domain.

Thus, one can treat any locale as either interactive or separate from the lineage of consciousness or associated and connected, that it must act according to its degree of connection. Here, structural domains instinctively create a corporal structure that overly compensates for its specific association with conscious substance; not as a self-conscious entity but as a fabrication that extracts from a system without its proper participation. We also have simpler domains, such as satellites, but as far as imaginative structural connections are concerned, the locale has the final say.

Overcompensated Corporal Structure

If one enters an overcompensated corporal structure without a self-conscious remedy, like that of an amusement park, they may recognize its separation and distinction, allowing it to act as an interactive space. However, its structure acts in a different manner, distinctly siphoning from a conscious connection to recreate such in a more formatted version.

The same can be said for the psyche, where one can create the illusion that the permutations and transactions of the psyche are part of an interactive system that does not connect to the lineage of consciousness. The problem is that one carries a memory of consciousness, and when an emanation occurs, the active, interactive focus of the psyche, the material with which one engages, has no remedy if it is perceived as separate from genuine consciousness.

This is because the memory source and its emanation are directly connected, any further complacency of separation is considered fabrication. Even if one could forget memory sources, they still remain in emanation. Whatever corporal entity they may adhere to will be strictly connected and associated with the conscious substance, activating in a dramatic manner and recreating that lineage of consciousness without adhering to its proper connections. Even if one chooses to forget the memory, it remains an emanation so long as they retain an imprint of that conscious substance.

Memory's Tie to Consciousness

This is why one can no longer enact the psyche as if it is an interactive locale separate from consciousness; it will always participate in that emanation. The amusement park cannot be structurally connected to a city and still order itself to the tenth degree to create an interactive experience, e.g. trees and foliage. It requires a structural disconnection before it can border itself and create its fantastical aspects. This is despite its self-conscious recognition to act more of a fantasy than reality.

However, we notice that amusement parks are mostly opened in the summer, in which conscious permeation is most prevalent. As such, it does require a structural connection, but not in a manner of close approximation, rather, one that allows for a conceptual bridge. This is the answer to an interactive locale that seeks to act as an interactive base despite its structural connection, requiring a certain material distance while still maintaining a conceptual connection that always allows recognition of its time and place.

The conceptual connection, for example with the amusement park, is the permeation of consciousness during the summer season, such that when summer culminates it feels as though there is no conceptual bridge. (During the winter it is not even a possibility)

In terms of structural physicality, there is only one choice in the matter: either create physical distance between the locale that seeks to act corporally and its approximation to the emanation of consciousness, or it must act in accordance with its alignment and degree of proportion to that conscious substance.

We must not agree that the psyche performs a similar feat, in which a structural disconnect is required before any ability to participate in an interactive locale; rather, if there is a structural connection, it must behave in accordance with its specific connection to overall consciousness.

Thus, structurality will always have the final determination, whether in physical structures or psychic systems. For the psychic system, once one enters into a true experience of consciousness, they will always be structurally connected to the conscious substance. No amount of forgetfulness will change that.

One can enter an interactive locale, but the entire experience is based on its connection to the conscious substance. If one attempts to create a distinction and act as if it is disconnected from consciousness, they are merely averting their eyes from the lineage of consciousness that they are experiencing within the interactive locale. There is a structural connection, and one is only denying its memory.

While there may be a possibility, I do not see it at the time of writing, of structurally disconnecting once there is a permeation of consciousness, we see that those who have obtained conscious substance have always had that substance haunt whatever interactive base they may participate in, allowing the psyche, whether by intellectual borders or some other means, to engage.

The only manner that can alleviate the pressure of the already actualized consciousness is to provide a contextual bridge. In any interactive locale, by simply contextualizing it and framing it in accordance with a sky-view perspective from the consciousness emanation within the local, it is almost as if one has never left the consciousness world, and more so, that one has never settled or resided in the interactive system.

However, this is not a foolproof solution, because the interactive locale is required to act as a distinct domain. A fully demanding context would have one almost not participate interactively, and thus not gain the embodiment it promises, as noted in other works. Therefore, a certain risk is required, such that one slightly actualizes the interactive domain enough to gain embodiment and distinctiveness, but short of actualizing it for the entire psyche, for which the contextual overlay is the proper gauge of that interaction.

One may enter an interactive locale that behaves as a complex system, where their conscious substance is temporarily put aside and everything remains interactive. However, the connection is still there, and it will always begin participation, activating the corporal system beyond its measure of scope in the pursuit of psychic equilibrium and systemic balance.

MEMORY, PROJECTION, AND CURRENT SOCIALITY

The access to memory for retrieving social sentiment may be presumed to be a direct pathway to contemporary sociality, but in fact, it is housed within the contemporary permeation of the current process. Because of this, all sentimental or nostalgic aspects are based on, and found only in, how they are actualized in the current arena. It may be the default process when one is faced with a dilution of current sociality, which they may retrieve from their memory of such, to project onto the current process. But, as in any case of projection, it is the circumstance of projection that is most important in the process, and the projection is merely the layer that adds nuance to the current environment.

The truth of the matter is that the memory base is already considered in current sociality however it manifests, and can be found through that lineage. One can extract from a current setting to its lineage that reaches back to the first notions of any articulation. Yet, even the extraction process is housed in current sociality, and can only be effective within the scope of current sociality, as well as in the way it is articulated in current sociality. The only reason we extract the memory of sociality is to further the premise of current sociality, which happens to correlate to that lineage. But, in any case of projection or reinterpretation, it will be met with degeneration, for the projection will fade as though it was never there, and the reinterpretation will eventually need to be grounded in a sociality that has been interpreted, which, if seen as different, will fade in comparison to current sociality; at one point or another.

A noticeable example of this is in the distinctness of individuality as it were in existence, where even the slightest movement will be drastically consequential compared to a memory of later-day individuality. To make this point clear: World War II is less consequential to current sociality than a hand movement of a child who will never leave their indigenous land. It is not an assertion of value, as much as it is the realization that current sociality is the only measure of sociality, and memory projection or interpretation is only consequential to that sociality. We could ascertain that many current movements can be traced to an evidential pattern from World War II, however, that is merely the articulation of current sociality, which can, in large part, be articulated in various methods, one of which is history.

History becomes a complex subject when we understand this aspect, for it would seem an articulation of the past, when in fact, will always be an articulation of current sociality. This would be according to an articulated lineage of past events. The historical setting pre-emancipation would have the emancipating aspects of its history with little consequence. Yet, post-emancipation is a history filled with historical contrasts of emancipation or lack thereof. This is not a critique of historians, but of the perspective taken by some regarding history, as though it were a learned subject of the past.

Longevity is another notion of an attempt at projecting a memory of sociality upon current sociality. One looks towards longevity, whether of their own body, their family name, or any other form of legacy, with some respect. However, such is only the reincarnation of a memory of sociality. When we find children with no interest or regard for the notion of longevity in any arena, whether for their bodies, lives, or materiality, it is because they are most interested in current sociality and have little to base a memory of sociality upon. It is only later in life that one becomes interested in this formalization, because of their projection of a memory of sociality, to which they would like to remain in current articulation. The only reason an institution can retain a memory of sociality is because it separates itself from current sociality, yet in many different ways, it is bound and housed in the engineering of current sociality. Longevity is another way of asserting that a memory of sociality should be prolonged as a projection, even when there is no regard for current sociality; it accommodates this projection and, in some ways, remains unaffected by it.

If one were to simply ascertain the experience of current sociality, there would be a dissipation of any interest in longevity or legacy, given that current sociality is animated and fluid, having no ability to be retained as it were, or to control its process of animation; very much the way a child views the subject.

There is another problem with a memory assertion on current sociality: by its very definition, it is the attempt to denounce current sociality for the ability to animate memory. In the case of viewing current sociality with a memory trace for articulation, interpretation, or projection, it is recognized as the core value of sentiment, to which the memory is simply a byproduct for that assertion. However, when the assertion is foremost as the criterion by which to view reality, current sociality will disrupt that procedure and, in effect, cause degeneration to the current realm. Yet, immediately following such a process, the individual or group attempting to do so will recognize themselves as an institution and become protected by its intrinsic makeup, which does not disrupt ongoing sociality but also has the ability to continue with their memory attachment.

However, in cases where an institutional backing is not recognized, it would disrupt current sociality because one is diverting from the current process to fulfill the memory input, all the while utilizing current sociality to engineer this effect. The political institution is protected by the very notion of it being a political institution, so that although it may be some form of memory projection or interpretation, it is done through institutional parameters. Yet, we could imagine if this were done without institutional parameters, the event would have one ignore the proceeding of current processes, all while using the "children" to engineer their ability for projection.

These children are the exemplifications of current sociality, as we have noted them being unable to ascertain a memory of sociality because there is none; unless we consider children of institutional systems, to which they are merely members of an institutional body, more so than what we typically consider the term "children."

The problem with ascertaining general sociality, especially when we realize that historical and memory precedents have little usage in the corporation, but only after the fact in determinate interpretation or otherwise, is only available in the case of embeddedness to general sociality. This would mean that one must relinquish those precedents in order to facilitate true corroboration, in the way a child ascertains sociality merely from the vantage of no other formation. Adulthood requires the separation of these forms and methodologies to gain access to the true nature of general sociality. In the event of corroboration, one is able to apply whatever they deem necessary, including historical or memory precedents, to then be integrated and offer perspective on that very notion of general sociality which was realized without its participation.

We find this occurring most readily with parents and children, where the parental perspective includes a formation of memory or method that does not allow the understanding of general sociality; to which the child applies themselves, and then the child is parented from a misconstrued perspective.

Parenting a notion of social prominence that does not exist within the child teaches a path that is automatically misplaced from its constitution. This is why the parent must leave all roles that they have acquired, all the memory of sociality, and all other deviations, to then adhere to general sociality. Only afterward should they attend as though the child is permeating a truth that has no bearing other than itself, which can then be parented accordingly: directed or redirected according to a projected view of the outcome in regards to society. It may be important to note that generating the notion of the child's intrinsic sociality may be a distraction from parenting, as though the expression of automatic goodness is the innate view of general sociality. There is no evil or good to be termed in general sociality because it precedes those categories; for warfare is both evil and good, and peace is as well, but only in the layered analysis which deviates from general sociality is that notion able to be applied.

In reality, if one applies themselves in proper proximity to general sociality, the adage of its direction, as well as its moral suppositions, are available with little deviation from its center. A child may react in their expression to the sugary substance, which without any other perspective might be viewed as their expansive development, and more so of that substance to follow that will.

Yet, without removing oneself from the occasion concerning health parameters and other political notions, one can realize within the situation its moral conjecture. For if one follows the dealings of the child regarding ingestion and activity, which becomes limited by hyperactivity or degeneration after an overburst of energy, or in how the child does not intake other nutrition and becomes transfixed on this food source, the realization is that it is not an expansion of the child's dealings in its fundamental experience; that is, without any analysis of the situation. It is merely the appropriation of form in general sociality that has not been viewed with required profundity, which is the cause of a degenerative supposition. We can take heed of that lack of nutritional analysis present in the process, or the recognition of the source of sugar being without a lineage of normal human consumption. More importantly, it is the lack of experiential knowledge regarding that sociality: deprivation of sleep, hyperactivity at the wrong times, diminished activity when attention is required, obsessive focus on sugar consumption; all realized as detrimental by the very experience of being fixated upon something.

A parent can either recognize that fixation is not a proper orientation to any area through analysis of such, or they can realize that fixations are, in their experience, a degenerating expanse, losing animation the further into fixation one goes.

THE MEMORY–SOCIALITY GAP

The gap between memory and general sociality will always exist, as the development of general sociality alongside memory is not confounded. We cannot expect it to be cumbersome if it were the reverse. The imprinting of memory is not entirely based on an encapsulation of general sociality because one is fluid and the other is solid, and the transition itself is founded on differing modalities of interpretation. Even if we could access the ambivalent nature of general sociality that is confounded in memory, it will be contrasted with another form of general sociality that arrives later. The only way to encode a memory is to remove oneself from general sociality, to then assert a distinctive role; it is common to generalize an entire generation by a certain perspective, because in fact, there was a process of encoding that had them remove themselves from the consisting fluidity of general sociality. That is, one must take a stance in some criteria or another, and already in that position, there is a gap in which general sociality continues onward.

The attempt to mend that gap is futile, as though it would be the case of trying to mend father and son into one cohesive unit; the distinctiveness of each side is meant to be so. One can reconcile two distinct memories by way of a conceptual overlay, "this generation is responding to this generation." However, this is not the factual lineage, for the child or a later memory is distinct and based on the general sociality of its current moment; which is not a response to anything other than animating according to the current environment.

The conceptual overlay seems promising: a generation of war has the succeeding generation dislike war, or a traumatic memory has the next possibility of a similar experience to be avoided. But this is merely the projection of one memory upon current sociality, with negligence toward its true nature. The generation of willingness for peace is not responding to its current sociality but merely to how they view the preceding memory, which they have projected upon their current experience. It is usually the case, that is, for traumatic memory to do such, because it is a memory that has suitable sentimentality that would seem like something not to ignore. That is, the generation of posturing peace is unable to move past the memory preceding them, such that they are fully ingrained in its narrative structure, as though it would appear to be a true form of sociality.

This is the very catastrophe of war or traumatic memory, where it not only disrupts the current moment, and in the case of war, its destructive material pathway, but also that its memory lingers, causing the succeeding constituents to follow the memory and neglect the fluidity of general sociality. In that case, general sociality takes a hiatus while the memory continues to be projected, and only when that process is void, does general sociality take its case again.

To be clear, there is always a subliminal form of general sociality, for any form of projection of memory must be engineered as a process based on current sociality. However, that form of subliminal sociality is subdued, and is difficult to notice because of the insistence of that memory projection.

For example, the generation proceeding war, which although posturing peace, was contained by a controlled sociality that might be in regard to any number of aspects. To take this a step further, the generation of war, or the current experience of trauma, is also deviating from general sociality, in that although it is the most egregious version of its encapsulation, it goes beyond and neglects the process of fluidity that manifests this form of sociality.

For example, we need not look far to notice that World War II was merely an encapsulation of the philosophy of technology in relation to human value, which was very current and had nothing to do with war. We often overlook this because of the catastrophe of war, but it is the case that they were performing a scientific experiment, with and in how it was responded to.

This is why, in the case of succeeding traumatic memories, one is most adept at ignoring its symptomatic urges as well as all its sentimentality, not so much for repression but to notice the fluidity of general sociality of their psyche that proceeds from that event. Over time, it can be incorporated with small measures, such that the narrative is not revolved around a specific memory, as well as to proceed from that event.

The memory cannot be processed by itself but needs more general sociality for that performance, which, in the event of focusing on that process, will neglect general sociality and have the individual become embedded in that formation of memory. By default this cannot be processed as there is no continuance to the memory, as though there is no animation past the memory but still is following the disagreement of memory and its assumptions. In this case, there is no solution, as all possibilities are barred.

This is another difficulty found in war, if to relive the memory, then war continues in various forms and is problematic. And if to succeed from war, then it may be projected. This would cause general sociality to not continue as it were, as well, having war not confounded in its process as a memory based on a continuing narrative.

Corporal System as a Custodian of Social Memory

The corporal entity not only serves as a redemptive force of sociality but is also dependent on that very sociality by which it finalizes its system. In this way, the corporal structure can be seen as the harbinger of sociality for a given duration, in that it can contain sociality at its fundamental level and carry it through periods in which sociality does not fully extend itself. To be the one in service to sociality, it performs the foundational task of providing aspects of sociality, and it does so by way of memory, through which it extracts the memory base of that original sociality and offers it as a systemic approach onto that mutative form of sociality.

However, this is only true when it finalizes itself as a formative system, one which relies on a limited form of sociality, but still to some extent a concurrent form of sociality. When that dissipates as well, the entire conceptual system shifts, such that if the corporal system is deprived of stimulation, it then relies more heavily on its internal mainframe, that of the sociality of its system based on its members themselves, thus becoming more of an institutional aspect. In that case, it can alienate itself from regular sociality, because it is institutionalized in a manner that cannot be readily extracted back into sociality. This is because it differentiates itself in order to gain access to sociality in the first place, and that pattern of differentiation does not allow for reintegration.

For example, a psychiatric institution is separated from broader social systems, and in such a case will not be in a position to be retracted into sociality because of the various forms of differentiation required of such an institution. It therefore does not have a place to be reintegrated into the system. In this way, the institutional system is not an offering of concurrent sociality in any regard, but is only available in a particularized form to its institutional members. Those members may then extract information when later participating in sociality, but not directly from the institution to general public. Rather, it occurs individually, within themselves, at a later stage of public experience, having extracted information that was not privy to regular sociality but was so within the institutional marker, especially because the superego has been penetrated at that level of distance from regular sociality.

Imagination as the Foundation of Technology

We need to replace the euphemism of "Technology" with "imagination" because it is not simply a conceptual bridge between sociality and the environmental infrastructure but a manner of approach towards conceptual frameworks that are already imaginary. This means that imagination facilitates the entire technological framework more so than just the faculties of mind that participate in regular conceptual frameworks.

For example, the homebody or corporation are both foundational infrastructure frameworks and thus conceptual. There is a conceptual overlay that layers upon the corporation or homebody, doing the due diligence of creating an interactive sphere or criteria to which regular psyche material is received. This would be a rough definition of a conceptual buildout. Yet, technology does not simply do justice by providing a conceptual overlay because, in itself, it is a conceptual overlay.

When we look at a technological device, we are not perceiving something fundamental but have already begun the dialogical pattern of participating in a conceptual worldview. This worldview facilitates a small portion of that conceptual arena. When a technological device is in use, one is engaging in the broader conceptual framework which they are embedded in. Whether it is technology within a home or a workplace, it heightens the experience of those spaces. A device in a family home enhances the experience of a home, just as a plethora of devices in a workplace heightens the experience of a corporation. This is the picturesque experience of a corporation in the present moment.

Technology then proceeds to enter into communion with a conceptual framework in its detail. In the corporation, it is within the framework of the corporation and its details, especially tied to the imaginative aspects of that framework. All technology has the clause of participating in a preceding conceptual framework, which now attends to the imaginative elements of that environment. The entire scope of technology's potential lies in its ability to provide the imaginative aspect of the conceptual framework from which it is embedded within.

For instance, a device in a family home can only contribute to the imagination in a way that relates back to the family environment. Conceptual material is distributed to access that relatability in the imaginative realm. However, this information only highlights and accentuates the context of the family body. In the moment of writing this, I am found within the context of a family body, and I am accentuating an imaginative role that expands the horizon of that family body.

Even as we discuss a wide range of themes, these themes only provide access to the conceptual framework of the family body. If there is a weak conceptual framework for the family body, this material will be shaped accordingly. The same applies to the workplace. Any information filtered through technology simply accentuates elements of the corporation. It mirrors the engagement with those corporate elements in their detail.

This is why hosting a friend or family member in one's workplace would be considered a breach of many ideals, while that same interaction through technology is then perceived as appropriated and even recommended. It is not these familial relationships that are being interacted with, but rather a way of imagining the corporation through the lens of conceptualizing their relationship with such people. This may sound suspecting until we notice a personal call in the workplace, which makes others feel uncomfortable only because somehow this call is connected to the rest of the corporation. If one is found to be engaging in unsound activity, it will be interpreted as the organization itself rather than the individual, whether from an external perspective or even internally, even if it had not been made known outside the organization.

What technology lacks is the ability to provide the infrastructure it depends on. Infrastructure only arrives once an individual settles into a proper formation of infrastructure. Hence, cafes, libraries, and other institutions become fundamental environments for the public because they offer access to a conceptual overlay in the infrastructural world. This allows technology to serve as a secondary measure, providing imagination to that elaborated conceptual framework. The weaker the infrastructure framework, the weaker the secondary overlay of technology.

For this reason, there are multitudes of constituents from developing countries who have access to the entire library of intellectual material, and yet without a major shift in intellectual development by proportion. Even as the information is now available, along with all its learning methods, without the primary infrastructure, the technological device can only mirror in its imaginary realm.

From beginning to end, the entire process is conceptually oriented. However, because most institutions and habitats are primarily conceptually driven, meaning they are corporate entities, technology is useful there. In places where technology is fundamentally a non-starter, participation in public consciousness does not require the accentuation of consciousness, nor the need for corporeal separation. Technology cannot do this justice, as it relies on infrastructure to begin the acquisition. Therefore, we have our premise.

PART FIVE: INDIRECT CORPORAL CONNECTIONS

DIRECT VS. INDIRECT CORPORAL SYSTEMS

Direct corporal systems are at the intersection of streamline sociality that happens to occur at that moment. Because of this, direct corporal systems are extremely vulnerable to the streamline sociality and are disruptive when the sociality is of a diminutive form or the corporal systems are not structured appropriately.

All this vulnerability is alleviated through indirect corporal systems, which do not follow streamlined sociality but rather as a framework of memory that is based within a historical precedent of sociality; such that by being reliant upon a memory it does not fall to the degenerate form that is possible in direct access to sociality.

However, just as well, it does not take the risk and therefore does not experience a developed stature of sociality; since it is based on a memory, and that memory is but an inference point of the current streamline sociality. If streamline sociality does not arise from that memory, or moved beyond that memory, or if there is a lack of intersection, the entire corporal system of indirect access will become a useless formation of detail. It does not have at its base the differentiation of sociality but rather of a memory that might be personable, and in that case would be beneficial, for one is always required to differentiate all experienced statures of sociality, whether memory or not. As is usually the case, based on any memory that is more communal, all that differentiation meets without any personal benefit.

For example, if a marginalized locality follows its political framework based on a memory of streamlined sociality of global consequence, and then discovers that the current sociality does not require input from that memory, or that the memory has been differentiated in another form, or processed in ways that make input unnecessary, then the entire country becomes a useless proposition of corporal development. We cannot assign purpose to the individuals comprising the country, for the memory was never a personal abetment requiring their differentiation in the first place; rather, the communal activity was structured as significant for a memory with no basis in the personal realm. Thus, anyone who did not separate at intervals within that system will find themselves following a corporal system that holds no utility for streamlined sociality of the current process.

An indirect corporal system has the possibility of changing its memory, such that it intersects appropriately with current sociality, and especially in the case of an individual. We can find that one day they may follow a corporal structure based on a single memory, and another day to follow it based on another memory. The communal activity could perform the same process, although it is much less likely because of the organizational elements.

Memory, Infrastructure, and Social Animation

The indirect connection to the corporal entity has the benefit of setting the criteria to administer sociality. Even the indirect connection to sociality is based on a lineage of sociality that reaches back to its uppermost status. Because it follows a different process, we term it an indirect corporal connection. For example, we may view masculinity and femininity, or gender personas, as one of the quintessential corporal structures. However, we will find that it is always based on, and how it intersects with, sociality. Even if one finds themselves distant from sociality, they will extract a memory of such and apply sequential perceptual aspects that will reaffirm the nature of that sociality to stay connected to that lineage. Still, we must view this as indirect to general sociality, for one, it is based on memory, and two, it is based on a procedure of memory.

Additionally, we have three levels: one of direct corporal structures in relation to sociality, where the only separation is that it is a corporal infrastructure which does not behave as sociality does; then, we have indirect sociality, where it is not connected per se to the contemporary movements of sociality but is based on a structure that could trace its lineage back to genuine sociality. It is not an individualistic memory extraction that proceeds to distance itself from sociality, but rather the infrastructure itself separates, such that the infrastructure cannot be termed one of memory. The foremost example of this is any marginalized country in relation to the center that houses the primos of sociality, where the entire infrastructure of that country, from every aspect, is a corporal entity that is indirectly connected to general sociality. This does not mean that the individuals and constituents of these marginalized states are extracting memory, although that could also occur, but rather that the infrastructure itself is based on a memory and is, as such, considered an indirect sociality.

The third and lowest tier of connection to sociality through corporal structures is that of individualistic extraction, where it is possible that the infrastructure itself has no relation, much like if one is found in a desert or in a truly marginalized situation, where they are not extracting from the infrastructure to accredit their corporal composite, but rather based on in what way they remember that they have connected to that sociality, or in a way of getting information from that center as to what constitutes sociality (such as news or other forms of expansive information of current processes), to where they apply through their personal memory base of that relation and continue the corporal structure. This is the general composite of the notion of suburbia, which is an attempt at true infrastructural separation, one that is based on desert-like status which now contains individual constituents who apply their memory of that relation to general sociality, to do as they see fit based on their corporal process.

The mistake commonly overlooked in the concept of suburbia is that it would seem as though it is an infrastructural separation of all variables when, in fact, it is based on a political sequence, as well as, to some level, an infrastructural sequence, such that it is not completely separated. Therefore, it must act as a second-tier connection in the way that infrastructure connects back to the center, but more so in the inability of individual extraction; as long as there is no development of how that present infrastructure relates back to the preliminary sociality.

When infrastructure does connect back to sociality through an indirect connection, it does so as though the infrastructure is following a memory of its relationship to general sociality and, as such, is consequently disingenuous of an infrastructural state because its entire makeup contrasts and correlates a memory of general sociality but in no way has any relation to sociality. We could see this in marginalized countries, where, although there is a complex embedding of infrastructure, because it is based on an extraction of sociality or a memory application of sociality, there is no point at which that infrastructure correlates or connects to its internal sociality or contemporary, fluid sociality of the moment. In some sense, it is considered as if there is no infrastructure, no constitution, and no estate that is existent, but only that its entire construction is based on a nostalgic existence of its relation to general sociality.

The problem arises when there is an application of contemporary media or the correlation of contemporary sociality that is thought to be applicable to their current infrastructure when, in fact, the infrastructure is extracting a memory of a bygone aspect of sociality. This is not of a contemporary nature because it is not in relation to the manner in which general sociality proceeds. It would be a mistake and an undertone of internal sociality to assume that either the infrastructure is genuine in relation to sociality or it is up to date and correlating to current sociality.

However, with that said, every corporal entity is housed within a sociality that then reaches back onto general sociality, such that its current process, and whatever tier it is being applied to, does have a direct lineage to general sociality and would relate to some contemporary aspects of that sociality. Even as it follows an extraction of memory, the infrastructure will still only obtain its vitality and emanation to engineer such a process based on its direct correlation to sociality. And we could find, in the process of that corporal structure, residue of contemporary aspects of general sociality, not just in how it extracts memory, because the entire sequence is housed in a direct connection.

This applies for all marginalized countries, to which we cannot find the contemporary attributes that are not necessarily related to the media information of such, but are the animation that allows for the proceeding of this endeavor in the first place. This is why the political aspects of international interest are of such importance, because they do relate to how they correspond to sociality, even though the marginalized states are, in fact, without a genuine connection to sociality or a corporal connection to such.

In the case of a disconnect from general sociality, there is the possibility, as discussed in other works, of entering into the state of the interactive embodied locale, which vitalizes itself from within itself, and is not in relation to what is beyond it. Even more so, it seeks at all entranceways to have no connection to general sociality, which is a figment of its process. This arena can surround itself with a corporal structure, which will ascertain its required sociality not by the general process of connection of some lineage of sociality, but by utilizing the internal animation of the constituents that participate in that arena to present itself onto itself. It requires sociality at any point, such that, in this case, it is the people within that corporal structure who view a sensibility of sociality based on their individual interactiveness; much like how a family will present itself as a corporal entity.

But differing from this, in this case, it is not only the corporal entity upon the general sociality of its internal state, but also in no way accessible to general sociality, which is usually not the case for the corporal family. Because of all these required steps, it is usual that the corporal structures within interactive embodied locales will be limited, because they extract sociality fairly quickly without replacement, whether from external frames or from the features of interactiveness.

Interactiveness, as an element of the psyche, is a form of sociality, although disconnected from infrastructure or general sociality. It is a form of animation that can be utilized as it sees fit for a corporal structure. The interactive embodied locale is evidence of such, animating itself without any connection external to it, rather only based on the heightened interactiveness of its environment, which serves as a loop to continue its structure. Its major vulnerability is that it does not move in place because it is constantly reliant on the continued reemergence of incessant interactivity of its constituents.

However, interactiveness can also be used in the case of indirect structural connection and indirect individual connection. In both tiers, it will be possible to generate a procedure that animates itself with both aspects, differing from the interactive embodied locale, which animates only for one side, and different from general sociality, which animates from the other side.

In this case, it animates from both the interactiveness of its internal social body and that of general sociality. It can act like this because it is in this perfect in-between, requiring internal animation to make up for its lack of stability and connection to general sociality to compensate for the lack of interactiveness; or rather the avoidance of extracting personal information at a heightened level while also receiving information of general sociality that is being naturally fed into it.

This is why we find that political institutions of various statures, whether libraries, postal offices, government offices, or enforcement and protection; all act with a certain animation despite the very fact that there is an infrastructural separation from general sociality. They do this because these institutions are highly socialized from their internal realm. In all these cases, it is directly interacting with the constituents on an ongoing basis, to which that extraction allows them to animate from their internal body, as well as from the nature of their infrastructural connection that gives them access to general sociality.

In the case of complete separation, where it is reliant on individual extraction, it is still possible to generate these institutions, but they do so either by the institution, becoming an interactive embodied locale, such as the antiquated versions of English private schools, or by the assessment of interactiveness in its internal body that parallels with whatever later structural connection exists.

It is also the case that, despite general access to general sociality, whether by direct connection or infrastructural indirect connection, it is possible for the corporal structure to be less reliant on general sociality, such that it can process as its own a base of procedure.

We notice this in institutions that come to rely on their internal process with various elements of extreme importance, similar to the political institutions that seek to rely on their internal sociality so they can proceed unabated. This is done despite the movements of general sociality, because they are, in fact, less reliant on that sociality. They seek to act as though they are indirectly connected to general sociality as to proceed to be as corporal as possible, but more so, as internally reliant on sociality as possible.

Because of this, it must follow the manner in which political institutions go, with every aspect of its structure socialized; from its architecture to its social exchanges, to its hierarchy of needs, to its elements of dependency, so that it can be socialized at every stage of its process, generating its internal animation. It proceeds as an everlasting institution and would not be noted as those institutions that seem almost political because of their continuing disregard of institutional procedure, rather, it is its own island of procedure, based on the individuals that make it up and socialize those aspects.

This is not a foolproof plan of perfect corporate order, because, first and foremost, it is not in direct connection, but rather acting as though it is in indirect connection. It is also reliant on the sociality of its individuals who make up its process, and all those individuals are based on the manner in which they connect to general sociality at one point or another, and then how those manifest in their interactiveness in that internal structure. Although it can avoid general sociality for a decade or so, the individuals who make up the process are degenerating based on general sociality. Eventually, it is applied to its internal structure. It is simply leverage, hedging its process to a later date, which, due to its reliance on internal sociality and the slowed decline, has a way of backtracking.

In other cases, where the corporal structure is in direct connection to general sociality, it will degenerate in accordance with general sociality. However, because it has measures of procedure to deal with elements of decline, as well as extreme bursts of perfect general sociality that occur at random moments, it will proceed to extract and behold for continuing energy. This will not be the case for the individuals who make up these separate corporal structures, because they are not awaiting those bursts of possibility or potential, and as such will be sidelined. In that way, it is at risk for the procedure of its longevity, as it has no mechanism of protection for the degeneration of its individual constituents.

This is the very reason why political institutions are very vulnerable to the individual constituents that make up their process. They are completely reliant on them, and those individuals are not in direct relation to general sociality; or at least not to the perfect moments that may be extracted on a moment-to-moment basis. These individuals will decline alongside the institution, but the corporal structure that has a reconnection to general sociality, as long as it has measures to proceed when general sociality is not degenerating, can be in the frontlines to extract sociality based on its moment-to-moment developments.

INTERACTIVITY AND DEGENERATION

In a perfect case, it is both aspects that constitute a corporeal structure and become able to proceed in both degenerate and general development: which is through the mobility of acting in cases of degeneracy to be available to the general pursuit of perfect sociality. In the case of degenerate aspects, they perform as though a corporal internal structure is based on its sociality. That is expressive of its internal environment. We can notice this based on the seasons, in which these mobile forms of corporal structures act in the case of winter through their internal enactment of animation. In the case of the margins of winter to be more available to general sociality, which, although based on seasons, are in and of themselves seasons based on the generosity and proficiency of general sociality in every concurrent moment.

The problem with corporal structures that are reliant on their internal interactivity is that it would be of a person who is reliant on internal interactivity or a familiar environment, where the corporal attributes based on that form of sociality will be perfected for the corporal structure but not for the general development of individuality, familial, or social development. If one is reliant on interactivity to proceed with a corporal structure, it is simply extracting from the vitality of individuality, not the fertility of convergence based on the social environment; as though we were extracting source energy from an individual's body to then proceed to the corporal structure.

This has the corporal structure reliant on this interlaced state of interactive extraction, which is based on a single notion of sociality that could be repetitive across the span of an individual's application. For example, one can experience anger for many days or any emotion for a prolonged period, to which we could place a corporal structure upon that anger or other feeling, but it will not develop as contained by the corporal structure in any other way than the very limited scope of that sentiment of anger and its source of how it relates to general sociality and consciousness. Its final outcome might be the perfection of a corporal structure, if there are many interjections of these forms of interactivity, but for the individual state and the corporal experience, it is not based on a complex development or distribution of sociality, whether by the individual or in relation to general sociality.

If one ever enters one of these institutions that are reliant on internal interactivity, whether political or historical, one will find that, although animated, the environment will perform based on a sociality that has no interjection between its states and is almost subdued by a form of bureaucratic complacency. It is as though there is some sort of sociality, some sort of expression to the environmental stature of that structure, but somehow it is as though there is this extraction of sociality to allow it to behave as it does. But when one seeks to interject and experience that environment at any level of formality, they will be met with a form of complacency, as though they have been tricked into a submission of social staticness.

This is usually the experience of general citizens when they deal with political institutions, as though it has this effect of provoking sentimentality in the entrance-way or in the notion of it. However, in the internal environment and experience, they find themselves almost tricked into a form of degeneracy, which is not an experience of social degeneracy, but an experience as though it does not exist but somehow does exist in such a dichotomy.

This is because the animation that allows such institutions to perform is through an interactivity that is very incessant and extractable, almost like a court judge extracting from the witness or from the one who is at their most vulnerable state, or the police with an offender, or the teacher with the student. It is almost as though they utilize these forms of interactive moments to generate propulsion throughout the system, which has then animated itself.

But it is that very extraction that causes them to form as corporal complacency because it is of no interest to these constituents to participate at that level, and they are merely happenstance to the state of that environment. Even legacy corporal structures of this kind act in this manner, differently from the political institution that is reliant on specific individuals in their state of vulnerability.

In this case, it is the general culture of having constituents become as erratic as possible, almost incentivizing a form of insanity to generate a propulsion of animation for that environment. In the case of a perfected form of this, instead of relying on erratic interactivity, as is the case with more of these degenerate environments, the structure will enact interactivity based on a distribution of work that does not rely upon specific individuals to become as interactive as possible; as in the case of a courthouse or a police station that inhabits delinquents or defendants. This will have every point in its structure become a social topic of interaction such that the interactivity of its people, based on their free choice or non-vulnerable expressions, will animate the environment based on its legacy programs and culture, almost as if it is an accepted contract between any participating individuals to provide interactive animation for the environment, as though that is the true nature of the work and the corporal structure is secondary to that.

A political institution does not require acting in that manner by relying on the incessant interactivity of people at their most vulnerable state. Rather, it acts out of an extreme interest in the corporal processes of its structure, to the point where everyone is expected to perform in the most politically adept and corporal manner possible. In such a system, there is little room for the interactivity that would normally generate the animation of its internal body. It is almost as if the institution demands as much erratic interactivity from the public to sustain its performance, while simultaneously remaining dependent on its own corporal interest in that performance.

Legacy corporal structures are more aware of this dichotomy and, as such, incentivize interactivity among their constituents to animate their performance as a corporal entity. Almost secondary to this process is the acknowledgment that such animation depends entirely on internal sociality. Weakened corporal structures of this kind, however, often reach for a stronger form of interactivity as if it were an inherent cultural expectation, to the point that the structure itself becomes almost irrelevant; a complacent system for the performance of erratic interactivity, akin to the reenactment of childhood playgrounds, with no altered status to proclaim other than the market-driven interest, or political.

At the other extreme, some legacy institutions display an intense focus on the corporal structure itself, with interactivity as a secondary concern. In these cases, interactivity is maintained either through an internal mechanism of cultural performance at every hierarchical level, or through an extreme reliance on individual incessantness to lend the structure a sense of animated life.

Indirect Socialization of Corporal Structures

The attempt at socialization of an indirect corporal structure based on an infrastructural connection, to which it is viewed as a general sequence of social experience, will result in one of two processes. One result could be the disenfranchisement of that corporal structure from following the social sequence as it were, but because there is an infrastructural separation, it is of limited stature.

The second result, and more common, is that it is viewed as genuine sociality, but because it is not such, it is actualized in defiance of general sociality. It is defiant because it uses the experience of that corporal structure as though it were merely a premonition or permutation of general sociality, despite the very fact that they are different. With this in mind, there is a debasement of general sociality in lieu of this pretense of character.

In the case of participating in general sociality, it is layered as though it is based entirely on the experience of that corporal sequence, especially considering that that corporal structure attempts to mimic general sociality as best as possible so as to complete that verifiable state of it being a general form of sociality. It may even be difficult to articulate the differentiation, since if such is the requirement, would follow general sociality and its sentiments. Additionally, it would take the convergence and apply them as though they were a part of the internal system, to then reapply that corporal structure as though that were a general form of sociality.

It would be easy to attribute this entire corporal structure with an infrastructural connection as though it were a mimicry and imitation of the genuine situation, but that is going too far in its attribution of what is occurring. Instead, it is housed in a direct connection to general sociality, although disenfranchised by the infrastructure to acclimate to its corporal sequence that it thus follows. It is not a mimicry when we discuss its direct connection to sociality, and even in the case of an individual extraction of its memory of general sociality, it is based on how they have acclimated to general sociality in that very moment in whatever direct connection that infrastructural environment serves.

It is for this very reason that one who is deeply embedded within nature but disenfranchised structurally, politically, and socially will, in fact, be unable to extract their memory of sociality, because the very process that would enable such an engineering is without its basic structure and therefore will be unable to begin the process. It is those who follow a methodical conceptual layer that are most often successful in such environments because they are not reliant upon the memory of sociality but rather the methodology itself; such as mathematics or other processes that engender the mind to continue its nature and process despite its disconnection from sociality itself.

Therefore, we are coming to the realization that it is not, in fact, the process itself which we must focus on, but also the process that enables the engineering of that process, which is as important, if not more important. The only matter in which a corporal structure can be of any consequence is when the process that engineers the process has a direct lineage to general sociality, and in whatever tier we discuss the process, it is embedded with a genealogy to a direct connection to sociality.

PART SIX: INSTITUTIONS

Institutionalized Infrastructure

Institutionalized infrastructure is the manner in which consciousness transfers from one domain to another, all through the hierarchy of its substrate and encapsulation. Without such institutionalization, there is little to do in accessing or retaining the permeation of consciousness throughout a system; especially when considering infrastructure as something that connects parts to a comprehensive whole.

What we call, in terms of institutionalization, is the parameter set to provide a haven of corporeal aspects upon an element of infrastructure so as to ignore its lack of housing within the consciousness spectrum, and thus obliviation through overexposure. If we consider infrastructure as an entity that retains all of consciousness and its elements, then it develops itself by its default way, and thus without the ability of interaction; whether by individual to infrastructure or infrastructure onto sociality, in accordance with its pedigree of awareness.

In the extreme sense, an individual's perception or regular sociality views infrastructure not as separate aspects, but as a comprehensive whole, where there is no separation or containment of specific entities that encapsulate consciousness and rather embody the notion of deficient housing of consciousness.

Such wholeness being inaccessible is for the same reason that the complete openness of the psyche to consciousness, or to any system, makes it inaccessible: because we first rely on the outline of a system in order to gain entrance into its specific parts. Without such, it is not a system but rather an abysmal state of existence; inaccessible both by its lack of individuality and its lack of containment.

It really is the proper noun of a setting of infrastructure, an alleyway versus a road, a bridge versus the platform, which, by its given noun and the institutionalization that goes along with it by its varying associations, will enable the ability to carry along the substrate across these various spectrums without dilution. That is, if each of these nouns does not overemphasize its ability in such containment, nor become lost as a considerable entity for its performance and regular infrastructure.

(Steven pinker, language)

For illustration, we could view a road and assume it to be so arbitrarily infixed on infrastructure, as just a simple pathway without any connecting elements, to which it then loses its service and its ability of containment between its connection of higher nouns such as cities, locales, and sociality, to which of course there is a certain containment of connection through such roadways.

And the opposite extreme, we consider our roadways to be the facilitator of connection between all things considered, giving it credence beyond its simplistic nature. To which then, instead of facilitating the connection between its hierarchies of nouns, it begins to deteriorate any formalization of consciousness beyond construction. Moreover, it does not receive any form of consciousness, because it is rather a roadway to nowhere; like a roadway placed in the middle of the desert without any origin or destination, which would not be considered an entity for encapsulation.

But not alone is the roadway considered for its purposeful institutionalization, but rather in which it connects to its other serviceable nouns; so that a roadway leading to a city would encapsulate more than a roadway leading to a local town, despite the roadways being similar in every other form of construction and materiality. The institutionalization understands its encompassing state so that it both serves to be separate as an entity and indirect to the connection of consciousness. It ensures that it recognizes its stature in connection with broader systems, such as a roadway leading towards a city recognizing its institutional stature as such, but still remains a roadway separate from the city with its recognition as an entity considered for itself upon itself.

In this way, all institutional structures act in this manner: providing a system in place according to broader affairs, and thus permeating consciousness beyond its spectrum yet enough of an entity to encapsulate and serve as a formalization of recognition that could extract a form of consciousness, rather than regular and broad exposure that is unattainable by individualization.

One may assume the solution might be to neglect any form of the hierarchy that is suboptimal so as not negotiate the terms of every level of its institutionalization and rather rely on regular sociality to provide those connections and associations; all for them to input into the peak forms of infrastructure and consciousness. The hope is that there is no need for institutionalization at that level of organization because it is rather the permeation that succeeds all corporal entities.

However, without the hierarchy of infrastructure in place, the access to consciousness becomes arbitrary as well, for it does not serve upon the throne of a kingdom since there is a lack of recognition to the populace. That is, a leader without a sociality to be led would not be experienced as peak-consciousness, simply because there is no layout within the psyche that correlates with infrastructure in accordance with its levels of encapsulation of consciousness.

As to be considered, the roadway leading to a city is also a formalization within the psyche of a lower form of consciousness which leads to a higher form; and thus, associations of the roadway would be in accordance with that level. However, without the parallel associations of these lower-tier institutionalizations, when one succeeds to the city itself or the higher forms of infrastructure, they will not parallel in association within their psyche; for it would be considered as arbitrary as any other system, as there is no sequence between subparts.

It is this very notion that has a person of stature begin to deviate from their access to consciousness, despite residing in the prevailing state of that nexus; they do contain the encapsulation of lower-tier developments of infrastructure which would serve as associations within their psyche. Without this, a hierarchy cannot take place parallel with the external form. Instead, they partake in peak-consciousness in accordance with the elements of their psyche that have been developed for lower forms of consciousness; such that they result in a degeneration, to which the peak is now accessed as if it were a roadway leading to a city.

The psyche is not exactly the exemplification of infrastructure, but we can be assured that the complex institutionalizations afforded based on sociality are in accordance with how the hierarchy of psyche access between its lower and higher forms of consciousness. The entire notion of institutionalizing infrastructure, terming roadways as roadways, besides its obvious necessity of conceptual organization, is about granting a level of institutionalization so as to serve as a formalization of consciousness.

This very notion precedes every format that begins to organize the notion of an institutionalization, accomplished with the effect of granting the layout of the psyche upon infrastructure so that they can correlate and thus serve each other.

We might assume this whole process is arbitrary, that infrastructure is institutionalized not for the sake of controlling or regulating consciousness, but more for the sake of conceptual organization. In this way, one assumes that the hierarchy of their internal consciousness can function despite the infrastructure and its prevailing associations. But in fact, when one learns that perception is the seat of psyche development and organization, the perceptual field must adhere to the same rules in external form as it does in its internal development.

If one exists for a prolonged, existential period within an infrastructure lacking such institutionalizations, whether residing in a desert or an underdeveloped social context, their psyche will gradually lose the capacity to engage with that complex infrastructure, thereby losing internal access to consciousness as anything beyond a broad, undifferentiated mode, without nuance and individual attainments.

The very reason we apply a noun to something is because it has been institutionalized, and thus is constantly in motion to be understood and exchanged at a different level according to sociality. A roadway in a preceding era is different from a roadway in the current era; all in accordance with how that institutionalization developed.

A noun is constantly changing because just as an institution is quite dependent on its all-encompassing stature within a given environment, it is the case that the noun awaits structural change in accordance with that environment. It does not change wholeheartedly, so that a roadway will always bear a connotation of some sort of infrastructural connection. Because it is institutionalized, it retains that level of uniqueness and individuality but still remains available to reconstruction, that a roadway can also be considered a habitat of connection between one town and another.

But all this is not our consideration; rather, it is according to sociality that is afforded to this institution that causes it to gain its stature. As with irregular institutions, its level of stature is based on the affordance of general sociality, especially broader sociality, and it will be determined by that very perception. Although it is institutionalized with a distinct identity, it is nonetheless institutionalized and thus part and parcel of the broader spectrum.

Specialized Institutionalization

This is a form of the corporal entity which does not allow permeation of direct consciousness but does retain consciousness within its substrates so that it can be extracted, much like how a university does not retain a direct connection to sociality, but through its process of learning can access these forms of consciousness in any possible format, even more developed than general interactions with regular sociality.

This is proper if general sociality affords the institution a guaranteed stature among their own compositional society. So, a roadway is considered such not only for its connotation but also for its social agreement in accordance with its institutionalized state as both a noun and a proper noun.

This changes, for example, with a roadway that leads to a town, in which sociality does not entertain the institutionalized state of that form of infrastructure; that it does not gain its institutionalized status and thus would be considered a lesser form of a roadway. It lacks the exemplification because it lacks the institutionalization, although its noun still retains, much like how a low-tier college still retains the notion of "university," while the more complex universities retain the exemplification of what would be considered a genuine university.

The institution and its skeletal structure are still retained, but lacks the exemplification, for the sociality does not agree to that formalization but does so arbitrarily, for simple necessity such as directions or other utilitarian forms. As well, when sociality does offer a certain stature, it is according to its broader spectrum; that the roadway leading to the town can be institutionalized as the roadway leading out of the town, as a sort of exit ramp rather than an entranceway. This encapsulates the idea that the town leads to further things, rather than being receptive to broader elements.

It is possible that the entire sociality can misconstrue the institutionalization; thus, a town can consider the roadway leading toward it as such, despite the broader sociality agreeing that it is a roadway leading away from the town. But general sociality always cancels out local society, and thus institutionalizations are reliant on their most broad stature, rather than just a local notion of what might seem like an institution.

It is not general sociality that postures an institutional structure, it is consciousness and all its affordances. Because an institution is only the habitat, or corporal entity which encapsulates consciousness, it is most dependent on consciousness, not just sociality. Thus, limited or secluded consciousness would not have the effects to offer an institutional structure. In this way, we do not have general institutions that are considered complex and institutionalized in the fullest sense of the word when they are not encompassing the broadest consciousness possible.

We could even study the word institution as used in a negative connotation, for one who is "institutionalized"—to which they are considered for psychiatric disorders of a certain level that require the state's intervention to provide institutionalization. In some sense, we are applying this term to be placed upon a human psyche so that they retain whatever measure of consciousness they do contain in a manner that would allow them to function on some level; thus, they require the full institutionalization of themselves rather than considering their internal mechanisms.

In its negative connotation, institutionalization is the requirement at the behest of a natural pronouncement of consciousness which is disruptive in a manner that requires a complex corporal entity, an entity of such effect that it does not allow general permeation of consciousness. Thus, it is usually associated with the medical industry or complex scientific experimentation, in which any succession of consciousness is considered threatening due to its sensitivity and internal state.

It is so open to any form of consciousness that it risks disruption, which in turn demands an even stronger institutional framework to contain it. In this way, it is not the notion of the institution itself that is disruptive in disallowing consciousness, but rather that it is required in order to develop and protect the internal state of what resides within the institution. Even a slight encapsulation of direct consciousness could cause deviation.

Rather, it is also the case that institutionalization, in this context, the connection to broader sociality, is required so that the institution can contain the information necessary to provide its internal state with the habitat for development. We cannot have a medical institution too far removed from general sociality, because it requires complex intellectuality to sustain its structure.

In this way, it becomes heavily institutionalized by its own direction: unwilling to separate from sociality because it requires complex intellectuality, but also needing to retain its own parameters as a system that has no direct connection to consciousness. Any such connection would be devastating to its structure, like a psychiatric patient re-entering general sociality, or a complex scientific experiment being exposed to broader public influence. Both would be destabilizing, either for the patient's development toward autonomy, or the experiment's requirement for an isolated, controlled habitat before it can eventually return to sociality in a proper form.

The negative connotation that is usually afforded to such levels of institutionalization might stem from a lack of understanding, either of the necessity of institutions or of the complexity in direct exposure to consciousness. For the inpatient of a psychiatric system, to offer them direct exposure to consciousness would be a reflection of their current affliction than any process of healing.

Likewise, the laboratory that performs experimentation gaining direct access to current consciousness will either be misunderstood by general sociality for its deviation from current affairs, or will succumb to its own pressure by recognizing its stature in a broader system; specifically, how it deviates in accordance. Experimentation would not be possible if it were viewed through the eyes of general sociality, because it is attempting to make possible what would be futuristic necessities of sociality, or vulnerabilities of sociality that are not necessarily displayed.

However, the negative connotation does have some credence because it both relies heavily on its stature among general infrastructure and is institutionalized at a level that avoids all direct connection. It must have a pathway of indirect connection, or else it may collapse into institutionalized methodology in itself.

Institutionalized mentality, in its intrinsic philosophy, is rather cut off from consciousness or all considerations of consciousness, while still performing with a base of vitality directed toward a specific aim or constitution. This very credence is applicable to many of the more malevolent elements in society, where one is given the right to detach from consciousness while still retaining some form of connection, so that they may act as they see fit, according to a generalized constitution.

In this way, both the psychiatric institute and the laboratory require a development wherein indirect sociality gains some form of access. For if, by a lack of indirect association, they begin to follow only their internal constitution without consideration of consciousness and sociality, they will still perform as if vitalized. Even without indirect connection, there remains some form of connection at some level of organization, as these are structured habitats within a broader sphere.

However, they lack the ability to perform at that nuanced level where the constitution itself gains precedence. Thus, if the constitution for the psychiatric patient is healing, it may be pursued at all costs; or, if it is the laboratory, it may be experimentation at all costs, without any level of parallelization between the institution and sociality, due to the absence of indirect connections.

This becomes even more problematic because both institutions inherently require seclusion due to their internal nature. The psychiatric patient cannot be given full freedom, leading to an encasement and separation by default. Similarly, the laboratory must prevent access at every level, particularly if it is biological, therefore incentivizing the disinheritance of any indirect connection.

With this in place, it becomes crucial to ascertain a form of indirect sociality, so the institution can function in a manner that still retains proper organization. Even indirect connection, by its very nature, must remain indirect, adding to the problem, since the institution is already incentivized to disassociate; there must be an avenue by which indirect sociality enters and exits. This allows the institution to remain in parallel with the structure of broader sociality, ensuring that experimentation does not deviate too far from the social structure despite its prevailing nature of performance and its potential or vulnerability.

In the case of the psychiatric patient, this is necessary for their development and performance as a social being, and also must remain in accordance with the rights and justice that would be afforded were general sociality involved, despite prevailing wisdom and the internal institution suggesting otherwise.

Might we say that the cause of degeneration within scientific experimentation and progress arises from this lack of indirect sociality? For it then adopts methodologies and developments that are not on par with any formalization of sociality. Yet it is not the social spectrum that has the ability to change its affairs. Rather, it is the internal state of the institution that requires this connection toward indirect society far more than the broader spectrum inquiring into that internal space.

INSTITUTIONAL FAMILIES: SIMULATION OF DOMESTICITY

The homebody can be performed as an institutional composition but differs from the regular institution or corporal entity. This is most noticeable in the fact that it is fairly vulnerable to general sociality, and only through a very dramatic separation of its social aptitudes can it be realized as a structured corporal setting.

In the regular case, especially with direct connection to sociality or that of infrastructural separation with indirect connection, the family body will need to recreate itself to act like an institutional version of a family body. If run like a corporal entity, then the family body will perform adequately, but we cannot term such a thing as familial insulation because it acts in every regard like a corporal entity. It is only when the family body remains with the composite nature of a family but simulated as an institutional version that we grant the term of institutional family.

A royal family, for instance, would not be an institutional family, but a corporal entity that happens to contain biological and social roots that almost undermine the proceedings of that corporal entity.

We find difficulty in matching a royal family to the institutional familial entity because there is much leaning toward its state-like organization. It is only based on the regular interaction with general sociality that defines a corporal entity, which, in the case of a royal family, is fairly separated; and as such, performing at such corporal levels is not based on its interaction with general sociality but rather from its internal process of sociality. It utilizes its own sensitivity to familial bonds and interactivity, which happens to be submerged for the effect of the corporal entity but then uses that very substantiation to generate the format of its corporeal animation. Such that it extracts familial sentiment to generate a state-like corporation, which does not rely on another external sociality for its animation, and is the sacrifice of familial sentiment for the goodness of its corporeal structure; which in fact has no direct bearing on sociality.

We find dismay at the French Revolution for its quest upon the palace, as though there was any connection to begin with, being that they are an isolated corporal entity that does not constitute any bearing on the populace, but then again, is essential for the continuation of a state.

When we contain an institutional familial body, it is placed in the vulnerability not of sequestering the familial aspects, because that connection is open to communication. The institution is merely the proposition of what would be a composition of a family body, and nothing else is added. It is only in the case where the familial experience is assumed to be "familial" in the sense of bearing a true exemplification of its sociality. In fact, it has undergone the development of becoming an institution, to which any social sentiment does not bear on the personal aspects of those in participation. Instead, it is only a manifestation of its institutional sentiment.

This is how a corporation expresses sympathy. Each of those familial members expresses familial sympathy, which has been changed from the genuine nature of familial sympathy yet still contains the very fabric of what would be a familial form of sympathy and not the version of a regular corporeal entity.

For example, one would say, "Hey, sister," as though this is not obvious to the true nature of a familial body, but in this institutional development, the provable sister, as though it is not the actual sister but one that is constituted as such. For this reason, the institutional familial body may find themselves unable to understand its relation to the environment, as though it does not match the familial sentiment. In the case of a genuine family body, the environment is one and the same as the family, and not only is there no question, most questions of its dealings are in concern with their embeddedness within that environment.

This is why we cannot view the sentiment of the institutional family body as articulating a domesticated sentiment of the environment because they are, in fact, not a formatted domestication. Especially in matters of domestication, they usually err in understanding its provision and properties since they are a recreated version of it. However, on the other hand, we come to understand domestication through the institutional family body, like a display in a museum, which would be difficult to come by in a regular family body. The regular family body does not imbue its domesticity, and might be the reason that little scientific research is on the subject of its nature, but only through the mechanism of an institutional family body does it make itself known, despite the fact that it is not a domesticated system but merely an exemplification of such.

The institutional family body is only possible when they are connected to general sociality but infrastructurally separate. In the case of the third-tier of complete separation, that is the case of a family body only able to integrate a true form of domestication, despite the attempt at performing otherwise. They may perform like a corporal entity, akin to a royal family, but that would not constitute an institutional family body and has no bearing on the family subject.

In the case of infrastructural attachment to general sociality, the family body does not have the ability to perform as an institutional model because the structural connection would seep into the familial aspects. If attempted to separate, as would most corporations, they would need to adhere to a general corporal model because they are unable to access the familial undertone without it being affected by general sociality.

With that effect, the family will take on a representation of participation in that realm and would lose all corporal structures. In the case of infrastructural separation, the environment is assisting in that specialization so they can become vulnerable to the true nature of the familial sentiment, without the worry of usurping general sociality, which is, in fact, separated at the moment.

To mention general sociality: individuals become part of a social environment such that the constituents forming a family, including familial entities, exist only if there are domestic aspects. Without these, there is no family body, because nothing familial or interactive exists in that environment. To engage in something interactive, it must be separate from general sociality.

Corporal and Conceptual Frameworks

It is important to acknowledge the differences of the corporal system and that of the conceptual framework toward a point of sociality, or in reference to sociality. The corporal system is a distinct and internal system that recreates itself based on an aspect of sociality, as though the point of sociality is its constitution. The conceptual framework leads towards an understanding of sociality, but it is not an internal system. It is simply an aggregation of information towards social systems. If we construct a conceptual framework or a conceptual outlook towards sociality or social systems, we are not manifesting the relation between sociality and its recreation, but rather a direct correlation of social manifestation.

Social sequence is lacking differentiation, and intellectual frameworks provide differentiating mechanisms towards acquiescing that point of sociality. It is very possible to construct what would be an assumed corporal system, or an institution for that matter, which in its day-to-day practice is merely the aggregation of conceptual process towards social aspects. The corporal system is not interested in a conceptual framework. It is not interested in how that intellectual material manifests towards the social point. It is sequestered from social reality and works within its internal mainframe to manifest its intellectual database. It is sought to diffuse from social interest, in the case of an institution, more completely, and in the case of the corporal system, less so.

Even in a corporal system that pertains to indirect sociality, it would still be, according to the process by which it has entered, social. It is not pertaining to how it seeks out social aspects, and how it receives the corporal system as a reciprocal of social process at any level of its organization; even an institution acts in that manner. However, a conceptual framework in its various manifestations is not reciprocal, but rather is a direction towards sociality. For instance, in a digital landscape, it is more inclined to be a conceptual perspective of a social point rather than a corporeal manifestation, and is lost to the corporeal approach as a whole. It is directly attuned to a point of sociality, whatever that point may be at the moment, and whatever that conceptual perspective effectuates. It might be termed alongside the corporal system as though it is considered work or other forms, but it is merely an aggregation of corporal systems to be applied to a simple conceptual framework.

Though this would seem like an advantageous process of systems, it is to its detriment because conceptual frameworks that directly interact with sociality are merely aggravating social points rather than directing or differentiating those social points. Because the social aspect is influential to all its conceptual connections, it will overtake whatever conceptual information takes effect in order to facilitate that social happenstance. One is not gaining knowledge per se or developing a conceptual ideation, more so than enlarging a social point or social aspect; information that is additional to that premise. The direction that one takes in the practical manifestation of that information will be according to that social point, and if we remove that social point, the information is lost alongside it.

For example, in the medical field, if one were to approach the subject directly as a point of sociality, that is, to heal and direct measures of healing towards the social realm, but specifically enchanted as an informational mechanism towards the ideation of the value of a social being or in reference to its equality across the spectrum—and if we remove that social value, then we lose the knowledge pertaining to that social point. We are only enlarging this point of knowledge based on its reference of social information in how one can gain access to that point of value.

Yet, if we remove that point of value, for instance, a marginalized or remote setting that is structurally and conceptually separate from central civilization entities, it will not be applied with that knowledge base as though they are not social beings that are to serve a rank of medical knowledge. It would only be applied as a medical development according to what could be conducive to the social value of a being according to a civilized system. And as we move away from that system, its medical intellectia is lost to a performative function, as though they are not human, at least not in a civilized sense, and thus unavailable to the intellectual mainframe of that intellectia.

This is highly contrasted with the development of the medical field through the ages, in that it was primarily institutionalized so that a doctor is almost equal in their performance, whether in the center of civilization or in any marginalized setting. It is the doctor who travels, not the patient, because the doctor contains the information based on an institutionalized process that is sequestered from sociality and thus can be applied equally in whatever setting.

The conceptual approach to sociality is thus not defined as a framework per se, as we constantly utilize it as terminology, but more so as amplified sociality. The framework is not illustrative enough of what is occurring is somehow separate from a social point, but is rather unable to be defined as a framework in itself and is based in every way on a social point. This is why the adjustment of a corporal system through a conceptual framework, or, as we have mentioned would be disadvantageous to the process of sociality because it is not contained by itself. It is merely amplifying points of sociality which, in some respect, do not require amplification or are, more so, disruptive in their amplification.

The digital approach of the corporal system would constructively be a conceptual framework vis-à-vis the activity per se of performing digital functions, which are conceptual reactions based on a conciliatory framework that is in reference to the corporal system, but is internally a conceptual framework that performs of its own accord and is indifferent to anything other than a social point in which it exacerbates itself.

The social point in which it exacerbates or amplifies is not in relation to the corporal system from which one is embedded, but merely based on the happenstance of that specific interest of the moment. Yet that amplification of the social point is in no way beneficial to the social point itself, since it is not being recreated in a corporal function or an institution for that matter, but merely as an amplification of social input. Yet the very amplification effort might seem beneficial to the social point itself if we do not realize that social points require remaining on a spectrum and in a sequence and its process of other social points. And in the stability of that social point, it is disruptive to social process.

If one constructs a conceptual framework directly interacting with sociality, it requires, as mentioned in other works, remaining arbitrary to its supposed material of social input, since one is simply housing social process, which requires its continuance to remain in perspective, so that the housing must be arbitrarily input to allow for the continued nature of social process, as well, to avoid amplification of a specific point more than necessary for a system. Moreover, it might be a disruptive social point in reference to the social system. For example, if one happens to be occurring in a social point in reference to something disruptive, which is now being applied based on a conceptual framework. It only amplifies the very disruptive element, which, in its namesake prior to any amplification, is still disruptive, which is now merely aggregating that very process.

However, there is an exception to this premise in that a conceptual framework can be developed to be corporal or institutional. The metric for deciding this is according to the constant negotiation between that conceptual idea and general sociality. Additionally, the development of that idea in consideration for being sequestered from general sociality, in which it becomes separate but also coordinated with social reality.

Even in the digital interface, it does not require remaining as a conceptual framework, although it is very inclined towards that notion and can be utilized in a manner of isolation from sociality; as though it is to perform outside of the social inference, developed according to its intellectual premise, and then reacquainted with regular sociality at a later date. If this cycle repeats itself in a scalable manner, then it will perform as an institutionalized or corporal premise, according to circumstantial factors. We can imagine this in a corporal structure where a digital aspect is utilized to adjoin with its corporal functionality rather than in its performance of what is beyond it. Or, as experienced in an institutionalized setting, a bureaucratic function, where the technology is an aggregation of its institutionalized premise rather than its performance of socialization. This, of course, can be applied on the individual level, where the utility of that digital function is based on how one performs in relation to that framework of reference.

However, there is a caveat to be relayed, and that is the circumstantial nature required for corporal and institutional functions, in that the corporal function requires direct or indirect access to social input and its real-time effectuation, which, if one is external to a conciliatory social process, there is no direct effectuation to that process. Moreover, if the performance of that conceptual function is unavailable to its connection to social input, then it is also unable to function other than in its conceptual definition. It is avoidant to social input, as is any conceptual framework, or it can be available to social input but is circumstantially unavailable based on the real-time access that is required of social convergence. In the case of the institutional function, although less reliant on direct sociality, it does require a division between oneself and an institutional premise or intellectual, so that it is not serving as an intellectual overlord, but rather as a controlled, sequestered realm which manifests intellectual material, while also requiring at some level a connection to direct sociality. In both of these cases, such cannot be performed in a private arena away its connection to sociality. One cannot materially function a corporal system that is structurally disconnected from direct access to sociality, nor an institutional function because it still requires some connection to direct sociality.

In this case, it is not because of an inability of psychological development, but more so of structural connection. Even if one is maintained at a regular basis in a corporal system or institution and carries that function to a remote location separated from direct access to sociality, it would be a conceptual function in relation to its institutional process. Moreover, it begins to degrade that institutional development or its isolation. In the case of a corporal function, it would be a conceptual relation to the corporal function, although well based on some other point of sociality.

In the case of a conceptual entranceway towards a juncture of sociality, when sociality has become degenerate or weakened, one cannot suppose themselves on any basis. Moreover, the intellectual process itself becomes weakened de facto by its lack of participation in the social element. What is left is either those that take the institutional method or direct sociality itself, for the corporeal aspect is now unavailable as it needs to recreate true points of sociality.

Sociality cannot make its way downstream because the points of sociality are limited. What is available is reframing or an ability at any level of intellectuality based on a diminutive state in its points of sociality, which will facilitate a continuing nature of its process. When the intellectual framework or conceptual framework are mimicking corporal structures, it cannot be maintained in its formal state because it supposes itself based on the injunction of social points; which are aligned with other social points, all in a diminutive state based on their limited availability. But in the case of any point of sociality, it is a mainstay of itself; it cannot be communicated in its intellectual aspect, nor formalized in its state as such.

In actuality, it takes place at a precipice of weak sociality, and sociality will acquire a different formula of intellectual interaction. It is not available to robust frameworks or dissipating sentiments, but to conjectures of the moment weaving through its process. It cannot be reflected backward on the stronger points because it is not a defunct state of apparatus; nor can it be reflected forward, but rather is reduced to the simple intellectual formulas that may concern the moment.

It is in this way that institutions are habituated in their internal organization based on a strong level of intellectuality that maintains an ability or conceptual formula of its limited level of social input. It differs in that an institution first sequesters itself from sociality to allow for an organizational structure, which then moves onwards to attain an intellectual formula to habituate the process, wherein the first arena of interface is that of the intellectual determination to lead towards a point of sociality. And if we are to be precise, it is the interest of a social point that finds itself useful in an intellectual formula rather than an intellectual formula finding itself towards a social point. If it were the latter case, then it would not be formulated in any other arena other than in a sequestered structure, because why would one entertain an intellectual process that is not inclined towards a specific social point? It is either for itself based on another structure of organization, or for a social point of inference.

Consequences for Simulating Corporal Function

To utilize a corporal function in a manner that would simulate based on a conceptual ideation rather than its corporal process has many consequences. One of those is that one assumes that the data stream, the intellectual acquisition, is fundamental and true to the nature of sociality and reality because it is not accessed through direct sociality or through true corporal function. It is assumed that whatever the details, it is conciliatory to social process. This is the detriment of conceptual frameworks that enlarge social points in which it is believed that the conceptual ideation is fundamental and genuine in its nature because it is attached to a true social point.

It is rather that the conceptual frameworks are arbitrary to the social point and it is merely a mechanism for which to interact with social process and is in no way a true form of nature in itself, more so an intellectual form of process. We cannot even call it intellectuality because it does not fortify itself in a loop of logicality. It does not counterpoint for itself, and at every intellectual juncture, it is bound up with in how it is engaging with the social point rather than the intellectual query of in what way it reflects its internal mainframe. Besides its dependency on that social process, it is unavailable to intellectual formalization outside of it. This is not to say that one is not able to develop the complex intellectualization through this process, however, it becomes beholden to the social point at every juncture, such that its intellectualization is infused with that social point, so much so that a consistent form of logicality is unavailable. That is, if we understand logicality as conciliatory points which lead from one to another, external to its influential measure.

Through this belief of it being a true form of sociality, there is an inherent frustration that accompanies it, one that is unable to piece together the manner in which it manifests within true social process. It is a beholden form of psychic material that has no availability for true social exchange, particularly in its differentiation, since it is bound up with social aspects and dependent upon social points, yet not gained an attribution that would allow for the manifestation of the material it has accessed.

There is a substantial amount of intellectual data infused with social process, yet it has no means of remediation from itself, nor any means by which other social beings can reciprocate in kind. One can imagine another being attempting to reciprocate by propositionalizing the social point in place of its intellectual proposition, such that the intellectuality cannot be accessed, as it is bound to a social point; nor can the social aspect itself be accessed because the intellectual framework is not considered arbitrary in that nature.

For this reason, when one engages a conceptual framework directly attached to sociality, it requires an extension toward this arbitrary nature, such that discourse becomes available to the social point within which the intellectual strata takes place; and is thereby available for the re-evaluation of a conceptual framework in the direction of that social point, rather than toward the social point itself, which all remains in service to it.

If one attempts, at any point, to place a positioned authority upon the conceptual framework as though it were conciliatory to the social aspect, they become disruptive to social discourse, and more so frustrating in the discontinuity of their social process, as though they are isolated and sequestered from the social environment by the unavailability of manifesting the material within social process.

Psychic Costs of Institutional Collapse

The intentionality and the succession between sociality and institutional parameters are almost as important as the structural division. As we have noted, the institutional parameter is distinguished from general sociality in that it reports its own organization, not corporal, as it would be if organized around a social aspect pertaining to general sociality, but institutional, in that it follows its internal logic, organization, and interactive base.

If the intention is to ascertain a continuance between general sociality and its associative elements in lieu of the institutional parameter, then, despite the structural distinction upheld by institutional organization, one will not benefit from the institution as a matter of its innate nature. One can individualistically connect their sociality into the institutional, or, for that matter, the corporal, setting only if they avoid the general parameters that are set between the institution and general sociality. Although they are animating the continual attempt of general sociality in the institutional setting and are actualizing based on an institutional parameter, because of their animation of general sociality to continue wherever they find themselves, will cause a continuing memory that will find representation in this institutional space.

If this is done structurally, then, in fact, the institutional parameter will be lost and will become general sociality, which often occurs in institutions that are usurped by general sociality. But this is occurring on an individualistic level, based on the intentionality between the general sociality from which their psyche and institutional setting are dependent. Even if they create a division and find themselves siphoned into the institutional setting in an attempt to continue general sociality, it will find what is required to offer representation to that effect, as though the structural and social parameters were not distinctive enough to create that general division.

A continuing attempt to purport general sociality in an institutional space will cause an individual to incite themselves to the depths of their psychological makeup, especially that which is highly interactive, impressing, and troublesome to the nature of coherent processing. The reason is simple. In the maintenance of general sociality and institutional space, the animating part, that which allows for vitality of the psyche, is institutional, which is the purportment of interactivity along a specific conceptual organization. But in the attempt to secure general sociality in that environment, one will seek to extract interactivity from one's psychological makeup to secure the high bandwidth required to maintain general sociality.

In a regular case, if one is a participant of the institutional parameter, then they need not provide much interactivity. The continuing organizational elements they encounter to enlighten their psyche, although divisive of the emanating properties of the psyche, allow the continuance of their procedural elements and general activity. But in the case of one who attempts to continue general sociality in an institutional parameter, they are attempting to utilize the entirety of their psyche and all emanating properties, whether in relation to its internality or to the external forms of sociality. In doing so, one is required to maintain strong attachments, as though they become a diplomat of general sociality in that environment.

This attempt at diplomacy for the psychological makeup will still animate itself based on institutional parameters, since it has been cut off from general sociality in its fundamental sense. Because of this, one is inlaid into the interactive aspects of their psyche. To become available to this type of abridgment, they must enlarge themselves as an interactive base. They must attend to all dramatic properties of their psyche to offer animation to this forum so that they maintain adherence to general sociality.

For the institutional parameter to process the psyche in a proper manner, it must take a distinctive portion that is separated from its general emanation, since it purports a high level of interactivity that would not be available to the articulation of all occurrences of the psyche. In the case of one who purports general social into that environment, as we have noted, will become highly interactive to the conceptual permeations of the psyche, having them explored at a higher rate; intricate interactive elements that lay embedded in the psyche, purporting high-consequence events and experiences in order to generate a constant flow of animation.

One of two things will occur, one, they will begin to experience prevalent psychological symptoms that take the place of their animating process. The psyche regales complex aspects that require a general and developed inquiry into the stasis of their habitat, as though it is unloading at a rapid pace to every crevice of the psyche, for which there is no available continuity for receiving in the information.

Two: they realize that they must stand in ideation of the institutional parameter, avoid general sociality, recognize that this is not an experience of an emanating factor or how it relates back to society or is distinguished from society, follow its institutional organization, and build an overlay according to that. This will compartmentalize into a specific arena of the psyche, for which only at a later date, when they return to general sociality, is there a complex process of dealing with the two realms: that of institutional imposition and that of emanating general sociality. Yet if one continues into the institutional realm as a performer of general sociality, they will meet psychological symptoms; whether a highly depressive episode, an extreme anxiety event, or other formidable psychological manifestations associated with the unburdening of a plethora of hidden subconscious material of the psyche, without any process of extraction or method for dealing with that extractive force.

THE INSTITUTIONAL LOOP

In this scenario of general sociality, it would be the case that there would not be an availability of acknowledging the social aspect itself, at least not in any institutional capacity. What allows for any egregious access of social points is its re-articulation, both at the event of calculation and of the social point itself. This is a double institutionalized process, since if we were to simply become institutionalized in an attempt to access the social point itself, we would be disillusioned in what way we have regarded what is altogether different, being of an entire overall and conscious association.

The social point that is prominent is first re-articulated according to the bandwidth of the institutionalized setting and is now available to exchange. This would mean that we are creating mandatory participants of the social point in order to facilitate an institutional demarcation. This may seem troubling to a social spectrum, for in one thing, it is the institutionalized predominance that takes part in a conciliatory effort of concurring society, but another altogether in that the social points themselves are re-institutionalized to force participating exchange. There is no ability to exchange with what is a different conscious approach. And thus we have the institutionalized persona or institutionalized social point.

What we find is that the social point will have, in its institutionalized process, the aspects of the institutional structure from which such reception is taking place and something which allows it to be distinctive and thus available for connection to its social fundamental. We might want to conjecture that it is rather an institutionalized effort to propagate itself, projecting its institutionalized stance, without much expansion of itself, being that the participants are arbitrary in this institutionalized form, which is already created by the institutionalized setting itself. However, there is still an effort made to allow for the social point to be distinctive.

We might think it normal to have an institution for institutional process which seeks to overwhelm and integrate social aspects, when it is by its nature sequestered from social process and is most formative in its function by a division of the social aspect. One primary reason for such an occurrence is to stimulate the institutionalized process by accessing social data for which it is either that the institutionalized process is lacking self-awareness of its nature and does seek social aspects as a natural occurrence for which that is the most amicable aspect of a system, or it is because it is seeking to usurp social aspects in order to expand its institutionalized setting.

The latter case of expansion is arbitrary, for an institution does not coherently expand; it only usurps more distinctive points to present itself as a stronger formation of an institutionalized setting. The institution of ten people in contrast to a thousand is no different in its social points, more of the multitude in which the behemoth of the institutionalized setting allows for its manifestation, irrespective of the social process. In gaining access to social points, the institution does not obtain more than it had before, because it only interprets its institutional and social point according to its ability of interpretation, which is institutionalized.

If we imagine the pinnacle of institutionalized settings, such as the antiquated psychiatric home, in whatever entertainment of social aspects external to it may occur, will simply be re-articulated according to the occurrence of that very specialized constitution and premise. There is no expansion in that regard, nor even of the premonition of expansion, since institutions do not have the will of expansion like a corporal or other social process.

Rather, we may think that the first point, that of lacking self-awareness, is the cause for much of the institutionalized attempt at articulating social aspects for its institutionalized settings. It is almost as if they do not wish to reinterpret the social aspect in an institutionalized form, and rather are seeking to gain entry into social process by way of understanding and being available to these aspects. They are compelled to re-articulate the institutionalized social point because it has no availability for denoting in what way the social particulars take place. It may even work over-time in the attempt to continuously extract social data for which none is forthcoming because there is an institutionalized premise from which it attempts access of social points.

In the regular case, there would be no access to social points other than in a natural social sequence. But in this case, there is a premise of availability to social aspects, but only in its re-articulated version. This becomes a feedback loop where there is a lack of self-awareness of the institutional setting, so that it attempts to access social points outside of it, which are thus necessary to be re-articulated for the institutionalized process by way of lacking stimulating aspects which compel it to seek more social points.

This is the cause of what we would consider an institutionalized expansion, which is simply the degenerative form of its misuse of that institutionalized setting. This, at the point of the institutionalized process, is not necessarily degenerate as an institutional setting, but simply misconstruing its process. But the aspects of social points themselves are fairly destructive. Social points are compelled into participation based on the institutional arising, which will be assumed in its re-articulation and lost to the axis of the social points themselves. Although in its best case, the re-articulation is irrespective of the social point, as it does not reflect back on the social point, as noted by the level of self-awareness in the social point. However, this is usually not the case, and one is usurped by the institutionalized premise. And thus, social points become repressed, disrupted, and unavailable for social sequence and its institutionalized overlord.

The interest of the social aspect, motivated by a lack of self-understanding of the institutionalized process, comes at the cost of concurring social process. If we put it at a multiple, this occurrence produces a constant influx of attempted conversions of social aspects for institutionalized settings, which help us motivate the reprisal of the true sentiment of that social aspect in lieu of its institutionalized sentiment. It is the case that in a highly socialized system, institutionalized precedent will naturally occur, since to enable social continuity in its ongoing phases is complex and as such would be easily met with institutionalized process; whether by the system or the individual.

This would mean that the individual becomes more aligned and held by the social aspects that they do contain, or the social aspects that they entertain. These are to be institutionalized for continuity in a social process. The irony is that continuity does not take place, since two institutionalized social points do not meet at any point of conjecture. If a single institution does not meet another institution because its constitution and its process, which it emulates, is altogether different, the institutionalized social aspect will not converge on another institutionalized social aspect. It has no articulation other than its internal form, and there is no understanding other than in how the specific institutionalized sentiment takes place. It might seem that there is an occurrence of convergence taking place, instead, the true method of exchange and continuity in social process is the fact of the social aspects themselves, irrespective of their institutionalized premise.

This is also the trust sentiment that is offered in institutionalized social aspects set against those that are not so forthcoming with a sense of security. One will behave and allow the performance of an institutionalized social aspect at a very high level because it is assumed that it does not contain the social aspects. But in that way, it also does not contain any concern for the social aspects themselves and is irrespective in regards to how it is re-articulated in the case of the counterpoint being a social aspect itself.

Although it is possibly existentially troubling, it is going to pertain to a true method of concern and exchange in social continuity, and there is no manner of simply remaining in one's position while the other social point takes an alternative position. All is affected by all, so that the effect is real, and so is its consequence. In the counterpoint being of institutionalized process, although there is no consequential effect, there is a concrete effect that takes place in that all that is socially concerning cannot be articulated and understood as such, only in its institutionalized premise. And if in continuity of its institutionalized constitution, then it will behave in a manner that one sees fit, and if not so, will move altogether to another arena. It is not found by the social aspect in any regard, and will move at no pace other than how the constitution of that institution and its premise take place. It does not even have the ability of reflection that should take place in regards to dealing with a social counterpoint. It is most threatening of all to participate in an institutionalized counterpoint, being that it is a system that has no empathetic or humanistic sense of one's social aspects.

The reason that it seems safer as an issue is because it does not even have the ability to manifest the sentiment of being threatening, by fact of it being the sphere of nothingness in regard to one's social point. What has no motivation, what has no intention, cannot be a threatening counterpoint, but can be a concrete and troubling sense of its manifestation in which a threat is not noticed and cannot be noticed, all the while to usurp at any pace with no change in whatever social sentiment takes place.

The interesting manifestation of this is that the intentionality is not altogether misplaced, but merely a misunderstanding of process. Intentionality of an institution to usurp social process is being unaware of its institutionalized premise, since the stimulation is the same de facto of its internal mainframe or in how it usurps external process. It is only the social points, from which all society including institutionalized systems are dependent, which are being disrupted. When we remove social continuity and its sequence, all other systems fail in their organization. They are simply methods in dealing with social sequence.

There is a buffer in which the institutionalized premise remains stagnant, all the while a degenerate social process takes place; for one, in that some social sentiment remains that is truly incentivized to be usurped, more so by the institutionalized premise in its lack of available direction in social aspects, so that time is doubled in the usurpation of a social premise. That which is the cause of the degenerate social sequence is now utilized in its degenerate form to continue the institutionalized premise, for which, finally, there is no social sequence left, and thus the institution fails by default.

Institutionalized premise does become available to continuance, being reliant on a minor level of social connection, as well as the participants who contain a memory of prior social process, which would allow institutionalized systems to continue for some period without social continuity. However, the moment that there is a complete degenerate form of concurrent social continuity, it would be the cause of institutionalized failing, since they realize, on some level, concurrent connection. If we press the institutionalized premise for their ongoing usurping nature, we will find that the social inlay that would default is to be a troubling form of sociality, since the individual participants and their laden sociality, from which they have commenced with the institutionalized premise, is not a working system and has not been for an extended period due to the continued nature of the institutionalized premise.

When we fall back to the social aspect that lay behind it, we find it to be so troubling in the nature of social continuity that it would not even be worth the material in social exchange; the institutionalized premise disallows social manifestation, and in that way, one is frozen in time of their social aspect to make way for the institutionalized premise, and if they continue with strong adherence, then a removal of the institutionalized system will be of the most degenerate forms of sociality: erratic, childlike, and disruptive.

This is the pseudo-psychological reason for the continued attempt of usurping social aspects external to the institutionalized premise, for it being the representation of how one's social repression for the enabling of the institution is being threatened by manifestation from social process. It is the social counterpoint which makes headway to represent in what way they have lost their social aspect, but more specifically, that it is manifesting by nature of the sentiment of that social aspect, and even more specifically, that it is understood to be unsubstantial as a social aspect in proportion to that complex counterpoint, and in that way causes one to be beholden to the social sequence rather than to this protected institutionalized premise.

Consequences of Institutionalization on Social Continuity

In the case of knowledge itself, it is the institutionalized attempt to articulate knowledge, which is truly the demarcation of social process in a conceptual and contextual manner. And to do such, it has to be re-articulated in its institutionalized form, that is visibly according to the reception of the specific constitution of that institution, but mostly that it does not *do* knowledge per se, but *how* knowledge can be prioritized for social presentation. This is an antithesis to knowledge itself, which is required to follow social process rather than to be the presentation of social process. And even though we understand the educational systems of knowledge to be institutionalized, this is merely to gain access to a depth and breadth of availability, not for the institutionalized premise of the knowledge itself. It is, in fact, the very aspect that is being avoided, which, if knowledge and educational systems are met directly with social process instead of being institutionalized as a structure, will be organized based on the institutionalized social aspects of the knowledge itself, rather than in what way the knowledge can facilitate a social haven; institutionalized as a premise that allows for such to occur.

In this, we are understanding a very important point, in the avoidance of an institutionalized structure, which will house a process that will detail aspects in its internal mainframe; one is now bound to institutionalize the social points themselves. In the case of a housing an institutionalized setting, the internal process can be articulated vis-a-vis a social process. Of course, it is institutionalized and thus sequestered from social sequence, but internal to its mainframe, internal to the educational institution, we can follow in all the ways that social process can take place with its mimicry, but also in its breadth of detail. In the case of institutionalizing the social points themselves, as though they are erected in the social sequence, instead of housing an institutionalized premise, it will disturb the social point itself by institutionalizing it, as well as disallowing for social process to take place under the rubric of that institutionalized setting. Since that institutionalization takes place at the point of sociality rather than housing sociality, it will cause a deterrent structure of the purpose of the institution within itself.

For example, if we take a knowledge sentiment that would readily be available in an educational institution and roll the shackles of that institutional presence, but institutionalize that premise in social process, then the articulation or the development of that knowledge is unavailable in any way as would be under the rubric of an institutionalized structure. It is already de facto in the institutionalized premise of its knowledge presented and available for articulation other than in its presentation of alternate social sentiment of its regard. It is the end of education, not its beginning, because there is no continuity of that piece of knowledge with other pieces of knowledge or external social process, since it is institutionalized at the level of social organization. This is why it is extremely important to set up institutionalized systems that house social process rather than articulating social aspects. When they house social process, they are available under the rubric of that constitution to move in whatever way it sees fit. But when it is institutionalized at the point of social manifestation, then it does not have that ability.

If we view the usurping nature of an institution over proprietary pieces of sociality at the subjective point of that sociality, there is no purpose to that institutional articulation, since the social point has no way of moving within itself. As it is being usurped as an instructional and institutionalized premise, it is being housed, but rather being housed in solitary confinement—housed by its conjecture itself, rather than housed in the availability of multiples of conjectures; it is a systemic oppression. It is the ultimate institutionalized premise that disallows for any organization other than the re-articulation of that sentiment for the benefit of the institution, which usurps that social premise. It becomes available for some level of exchange, but at the level of the subjective point of that social aspect, it is completely unavailable to utility in its institutionalized premise, more so in its social aspect being usurped by the institutionalized premise. Of course, one can dictate separation between its usurping institutionalized premise and how they experience the social point, but this is difficult for the institutionalized premise. At some level a communized presence of articulation of that social process, in which the nature of community had a presence of individual stature, it becomes a sense of dependency.

As the institutionalized premise fails to meet its social counterpoint, which in some way cannot ever be met, it exemplifies in itself the preliminary presence of the internal social point for which such institutional premise disregards. It is thus engineered as an institutional constitution that manifests this surrendered and underdeveloped social aspect as its coordinator of interchange. It is the last stage of what would be a continuous social sequence. Placed another way, the social imprint laid behind the institution, whether structurally or individualistically, is so inconsequential to a social point in the sequence of true sociality that its primary motivation is now protectionism from the standpoint of the institutional model. The constitution is thus changed in the institution rather than its proprietary knowledge of its system. It is for the protecting of the social sense for which one is aggregated behind its institutionalist premise. If we are in the loss of institutionalized premise, it is completely usurped by social continuity being of such an unadulterated version. We could think similar to a child's unconscious in relation to an adult, in which the adult will concurrently manage the social process of the child by factor of further mature development. In this case, once we remove the institutionalized premise, what would be children are now usurped by the continuous nature of adulthood which surrounds it.

If so, the bureaucratic structure is simply a parameter of institutionalized presence, nevertheless is another manifestation of the protectionism that takes place of the social aspects that are infantile to social process. The bureaucratic structure is the complete order for which no change can be made to the institutionalized performance; that is, it is a construct of strong rules, obligations, to finite and completely controlled points of access for which, in no way, at least in their perspective, can social sentiment overwhelm their institutionalized presence. At each gate, there is a strong order that has already been presented as the option of confluence, which is now the case that it will not be receiving social sentiment in any regard, since it is a premeditated institutionalized structure.

That is only in the case of direct social influence, in which the orderly function protects from a social exchange to enter the laden infantile nature of that social sentiment, which would altogether be usurped in an instant in social sequence. However, what it is not available to protect is outside its institutional parameters, so in the strong nature of its orderliness, it is simply of the social sequence to articulate that order in its function, more so in how it reaches back to that infantile social point. When we understand both the infantile social point as well as its protectionism, then we have completed the sequence of that social process, irrespective of its institutionalized presence. It is only institutionalized for its internal articulation, but in terms of social process, it is simply an adage of a protectionistic child, which will be usurped by the adult: in understanding the protectionistic layer, in how a child will be usurped by adult process, as well as the infantile nature of which that protection layer takes place.

PART SEVEN: SOCIALITY AND CORPOREAL CONSTRUCTS

Sociality and Functional Conversion

The conversion between general sociality and the corporeal structure is rather a natural process: one which requires steady maintenance to prevent alteration. General sociality is permeable, vulnerable, and indefinable in its raw sense, such that it only requires a simple change to its commitment for it to convert into its function within broader sociality. For that is what is considered the corporeal entity, one which acts as the format of sociality whilst being a function within broader sociality. Akin to a transport vehicle, which is not a form of sociality in its raw sense, for what does it imbue that concurrently participates in the happenstance of sociality, yet does perform as a function within broader sociality? Not in the extreme sense of utility, like the ground to walk upon, but more so to maintain an aspect within broader sociality which is embedded within the 'transport vehicle.' In fact, the very quotation of an aspect will constitute its corporeal embeddedness, or, 'the' to precede a noun.

For this very reason, personal names do not contain the effect of proceeding with 'the' or quotations, since it constitutes general sociality by the very definition of being a social being. The moment that a being becomes a part of the function of broader sociality, then we move into the brackets of corporeal entities, and it would then be appropriate to add the complementary 'the' or quotations, since we are referring not to them as social beings but as functional entities within broader sociality. Which, in the case of an aspect of their being that does serve that function, would not participate in this corporeal construct, or when broader sociality does not require that function.

The reason that the conversion occurs in a natural sense is the very recognition of the functionality of an aspect to participate in general sociality. Once such is noticed, it only seems proper to incorporate its construct as an entity, distant from the general sociality to which they had initially begun their succession. We would notice this in a new organization that will manifest from a social sense, and only after the effect that the public had coordinated with that social aspect do they begin to take upon themselves as a corporal organization.

This is the necessity of a conversion between general sociality and the corporeal construct, that there is agreement contained by broader sociality of the function to that social aspect. Without that agreement, there is no coordination between broader sociality as a service for the social aspect, for it does not require such part of the repertoire, and thus is unavailable for the social aspects to manifest beyond its general social sense.

We postulate a conjecture that any personal social sense would continue onward to be a functionality of broader sociality by virtue of the fact that one is a social being that is in participation of that broader sociality. However, this is not always the case, because a social sense can manifest from a source that is altogether not participating or in conjunction with broader sociality. Or it can be the case that it has already been provided to broader sociality and therefore does not require more functionality of that sense.

For example, in the case of a transport vehicle, by the fact that there are more transport vehicles required to provide that functionality for broader sociality, each particular transport vehicle becomes an addition that is not required by broader sociality. We may notice this during the early hours of the day where the transport vehicle functions in its proper sense, or in the case of limited participation of transport vehicles, so that in those cases, it will participate as a function for broader sociality due to limited resources.

But in the case where such is not particular for part of sociality, it does not function for broader sociality, similar to how parallel organizations of similar constructs in the provision of similar aspects for broader sociality cause a dilution of its sensibility as a corporeal construct. It is possible for one to participate with an aspect of sociality where they portray the functionality of this in accordance with broader sociality, whether or not it constitutes a mutual participation.

In the case of the transport vehicle, it is possible that even with a multitude of transport vehicles providing that functionality, one could represent (to themselves) to be the only participant or the dominant participant, such that they view broader sociality as a mutual participant of their social aspect for that functionality. Yet, the relationship is not mutual since broader sociality does not seem accurate, and we know so only because we are taking an objective stance on the subject and notice multitudes of transport vehicles, which if they were to remove their subjective stance, would notice the parallel offerings of that same functionality. Such that they must to make a decision of either accepting that their social aspect is not a functionality for broader sociality or to continue their general sociality without seeking a corporeal conversion.

When this sentiment meets an over-expansion of population, whereby the very fact of multitudes creates a vacuum to which only some can provide a functionality for broader sociality, the rest are not invited to mutually assist in broader sociality. Just as a transport vehicle by itself is a provision of functionality, but in its multitude, becomes diluted from the very fact of its parallel offerings, it would be the case in broader populations which can only provide some functionality for broader sociality in accordance with the needs of that very system.

Two possibilities could occur with a strong representation in the population: one, social functionality conflict, which in each instance, to perform their social sense without parallel and characteristic of another. This provides a stronger nuance that would be acquitted for function in broader sociality. With that comes the possibility of providing a semblance that agrees more with how it functions in broader sociality rather than the social sense, because after all, it is part of sociality in access to this aspect rather than in the proportion of its subtleties.

The second possibility is that the majority of the population continues to be a social sense without a corporeal conversion, such that they maintain ambiguity in what is publicly represented but retain a property which continues to endure population movement and general sociality, all without its converted representation. However, in terms of monetary proficiency, only the corporeal conversion can be constituted as a marketed aspect since a social sense without marketability is not participating in the market, although the individual themselves requires a monetary position.

In this case, we have a requirement for the corporeal system to recognize this disparity; such that it would allow for social sense to continue through a dispensation of its monetary function, more so to protect the conflict that arises in the corporeal conversion. This will cause either a dilution (such as a multitude of vehicles) or a manipulation of the accessibility to the corporeal function in contrast to the social aspect that lies behind that conversion, which can be as well diluted in a manipulation process.

For these two reasons, the corporeal system must attend to general sociality for the monetary profits, such that it would not be in the best interest of general sociality to convert unless it is deemed appropriate, or to manipulate its entrance into the corporeal system, as it loses much of its social aspect and ascendancy.

Representational Systems and Biological Dependency

A representational element cannot produce its biological counterpart, as it were, because then it is exemplifying an inefficient role since the biological counterpart is in itself affected by its biological dependency. At this, all representational elements must be a divergent producer of exemplifications for a model of conceptuality rather than for its inherent and intrinsic effect.

It is easy for one to dismiss the corporeal structure and its general capitalist mainframe as divergence of anything biologically related, as though it is somehow the monetary presence that has the systems diverge and thus dilute bare necessities, rather than the intrinsic makeup that it partakes within. Even a corporeal system which in itself is not representational to general society is a construct that is built based on a representational purpose, as noted, and is therefore in its helm that it must be divergent of necessity. It is the case that in any realm where necessity becomes paramount, such as food or water scarcity, all these systems fail to continue, for they are simply recreations for the purpose of a conceptual extension, but it is never the case that they serve their biological grounding.

They may in fact interact with a biological sentiment, whether in the case of a corporeal system which is beholden to a representational theme or in the case of general representatives, where it includes a biological footprint so as to proceed as though it were enacted for a purposeful endeavor. We would find it difficult to set a corporeal system that does not serve a biological purpose at its fundamental level, for it is then outside the realm of general interaction; as one would proceed without severance from the organism.

It is for this reason that the medical field is the highest form of corporeal structure, because it serves at the closest intersection of biological necessity, although it is also the case that it is not biologically dependent, even as it may seem so. It is simply the re-appropriation of the human organism into its centric system to participate in a meandering of conceptual data points that ultimately lead back to a provision of health; but in some cases are in themselves detrimental to the final biological purpose. It is comparable to the same relation as a mechanic in service to a vehicle, which, although in itself does not have a biological dependency, since vehicles do not find purpose in themselves, is rather the case that through utility the same is true in the case of the human body in relation to the medical field.

We have become accustomed to the language of success or outcome as though it were connected to its biological footprint from the onset, when it is in fact very able for a corporeal system to produce things even as it never participated in the true nature of social experience. One could only apply a thought exercise in placing a shopping mall inside a hospital, or specifically near medical work, to notice that it is not merely the effect of purpose, whether it is clothing for shopping or health in the case of medical provision, but because it is treated as separate from sociality and thus is disruptive, despite the very fact that it produces said health.

Representational systems must in fact be either completely disinherited from the social mainframe, as in the case of hospitals nearly entering into a political arena that proceeds beyond the state level or even global system, or is the case where there is little biological lineage but maintains its social connection to provide its much needed fulfillment for the reduction of its internal system.

Thus we see a correlation in which, if the system, whether corporeal or representational, is highly dependent on biological necessity, as in the case of water or medical provision, it would be in a state of separation from sociality to its utmost degree, even going so far as to require political regulation and control to substantiate it above and beyond social systems. But in the case of little biological dependency, as would be the case with the mechanic repairing the vehicle, it would be required to stay connected to social systems, because it is in fact less associated with biological dependency and is rather only the user after the fact; in the case of getting to a location which can even start the attempt of claiming biological necessity.

Because of this, we will hardly find an efficient mechanic that is not connected to some sort of sociality, and this is only the case when it is in relation to private individuals. However, when we enter into political systems, it is purposeful to engender whatever part of the system, whether vehicles or any other aspect, because the entire political echelon is a corporeal system that does not require biological dependency in itself, but is rather adjacent to general sociality as a whole. This is also why vehicles related to political echelons, whether public transportation or mail service, will always be prepared as a form of continuity within their internal system, because they never attempt to deal with sociality as it is, despite the fact that they partake in the same roads as private individuals. This is the very power of political systems, that they can create distinct separations despite common general interactions, such as mail for a home or political vehicles adjacent to private vehicles; because it is generally understood at every level that it is distinct and separate, so that it does not partake in sociality as it were.

VULNERABILITY OF CORPORATE ENTITIES

Because the corporate entity is but an internal configuration of amplified sociality in an enclosed environment, its most pernicious vulnerability is that of external sociality. In its highest form, the corporate entity might cease to exist because it cannot perform the amplified function of such height of sociality without following the exposure of that sociality; such that it loses the encasement of its internal mechanism.

In the situation of limited sociality, or little to no sociality, the corporeal function must be more encased in that it does not have much interaction with that small measure of sociality, and is more focused on its internal process of amplification of that measure. However, in the continuity of the corporal structure, despite a prevalent low bar of external sociality, it may be the case that it begins to act as an amplification of the measure of sociality that may serve against that very sociality. If the sociality that is allowed entry from the external front carries negative attributions or characteristics, that form of sociality excites the nature of the system.

Protective measures can be an accurate portrayal of the average that exists on the external front, and the result will be that the corporal function is requisite in retaining a memory of sociality that are not regularly permeating existing sociality. Yet, it remains dependent on the true form of sociality, such that its amplification of that measure might then proceed upon, in a scalable fashion, whatever negative attribute is present in the specific corporal form.

THE DETERMINANT FACTOR

The proclivity of one's entrance towards an object, arena, or realm is going to be the determined factor of its outcome. If the determinant factor dissipates, so does the entire coordination of the sought-out aspect. Most of the time, it would be difficult to change the determinant factor because the entire relational buildup which succeeds from it is based on that determinant factor. If one enters the arena of affluence and its status, but does so as their determinant factor for the representational activity or the thought of proclivities towards comforts and access, this determined factor will continue to define that relationship with little ability to change as the process goes along. Each continuing relationship with the determinative factor as the first marker means that all decision-making will be based on whether there is proclivity towards comfort or representational animation. In its outcome it is rather a disregard of affluence and more so a fixation towards comfort and personal animation in the public sphere.

This is not inherently flawed, because if a determined factor is the demarcation of war, continuing process, and sociopathy, such a development of fixation follows. However, because the aspect of which one is reaching out is understood as something more than these determinate factors, termed as influence rather than proclivities towards comfort, the individual is pressed into the ambivalent nature between their determinant factor and the obtainable aspect or system.

If the event, aspect, or system transpires based on a defined determinant factor, such as when one has no interaction or opinion as to the succession of an integrated aspect system, a natural determined factor will manifest; there is no neutral process. Since everyone enters a city or complex infrastructure without the ongoing internal conversation as to the terminating aspect of that process, such will be decided for them. This determined factor is the cessation of being a genuine participant of that system. There is no worth in the process of interaction, but more so the attempted experience of being an element of that part; instead of socializing that process they are becoming the experience with no other reserve in the foreground.

A common development of a defining determinant factor is one's entrance to the corporate system, to where, instead of it being in service to the general sociality of their psyche or broader sociality of the environment, they will in fact become defined by the ascendancy and degeneracy of the corporate system; all against internal general sociality and external broader sociality. The very notion of having the determinant factor as the corporate system, which is in response to sociality and more so, acquired based on its supposition itself, causes one to lose the process of ascendancy towards the pro-social system, rather relying on the corporate process itself; despite and void of general sociality, internal or external.

There is a determinant factor, and its fixated outcome is not because of the generation itself, but rather lies in the ambiguous nature of one's succession towards a single factor while finalizing the outcome of another. In a case of one's determinant factor being a corporate system, or career, it would be the case that it is possible that, for themselves on a personal level, they are unambiguous about the fact that they would like the succession of the corporate system and its entailments, despite general sociality. However, because there is an objective reality that the corporate system is a dependency and in service to general sociality, they will in fact be participating in the general degeneration of themselves, so that in the advancement of the corporate system they would lose, more so, general sociality of their internal psyche as well as general sociality of the objective realm; because the corporate system is put against what it is in service to.

If, in fact, the corporate system was the reality structure itself, then we could make the argument of its continuing progression. However, because the corporate system is completely and entirely reliant upon general sociality of the environment, and one having it as the only determinant factor, is going to disregard general sociality in favor of the corporate system. However, one caveat is honor, and in which one participates in the corporate system in a manner where it responds in service and proper orientation to general sociality, such that even with their fixating procedure, the calibration of the corporate system they adhere to will follow a sequence that will protect and serve their personal ascendancy. However, this does not fortify the distance towards one's internal general sociality, such that even if the function fits perfectly, a fixation within its domain is a pro-development for objective sociality. For their individual case, they will not enjoy that development at the personal level, so that their entire sociality henceforth, proceeding and succeeding their adherence to the corporate system, will not remain intact and will not participate in that development; such that they may be considered an advancement without ever having a personal participation in that experience.

Ambiguity and Degeneration of Sociality

The inclination of a determinative factor to contribute to the degeneration of internal sociality causes either ambiguity, where one assumes development in a certain arena only to be met by another, or general distortion, such that, embedded within that choice factor, it is unable to streamline access because it assumes, in a sense, one trajectory when, in reality, another becomes its manifestation. In the case of non-ambiguity, like our example of the determinate factor being the corporate system, it would be the case that one is then bound to the acquisition of that determinant factor in the allowance to participate in the overall sociality of their psyche.

In any case, if the determinant factor is preceded with prior fixating attributes, then it will become a devourer of internal sociality; only because it is reconsidered like any other fixation. We are merely discussing the determinative factor which is available to the participation of sociality, but because of either its ambiguous nature or its embedded natural framework that does not allow for relational activity, one will be drawn to the final outcome of that determined factor. This would be in the case without relational activity, to become an element of that environment, and in the case of ambiguity, to where they find themselves by the determinant factor against the more formidable characteristic of the other side of the ambiguous question.

In both cases, the outcome is undesired, because in the ambiguous nature it remains ambiguous because of its avoidance of that reality, and in the case of becoming an element of the environment, it would seem that no individual willingly wants to participate in becoming the rock of an environment rather than to be in relationship to it; but is the natural consequence of an undefined determinant factor. We have already noted that there is an objective formula to the outcome of a determinant factor, such that if it is of the nature in which one participates, and it always brings sociality, then they will, in fact, be dependent on the fluctuations and the remembering of pro-sociality in the objective forum.

One example is the corporate system, but it can be the case where one participates as the ideation of that character rather than the proposal of its sequential harmony. When one follows the idea of an aspect, for example, if in the case of affluence one is following the ideation of affluence rather than the material manifestation of such; they will have the determinant factor become the defining outcome, such that the ideation is without consequence to the individual's participation; it is an ideation and not a personal connection. As well, it will not participate in broader sociality in its platform, because the idea simply succeeds to platform itself in that environment; that it exists without any recognition of the natural habituated stance of its dynamic structure.

Although one would assume that in natural participation of their sociality to an environment would be the cause of succession in that environment, because the factor is undefined or ambiguous, the natural manifestation is such that, first, the environment becomes a believable entity to which all personality participates, and secondly, they lose their relational activity to what is permeable and more animated than their personal aspect; that they will lose their attainability to anything other than becoming a product of an environmental movement.

This very idea is the cause of most of the detriment that the immature psyche proceeds upon with failure, because it seems logical that if one enters by way of general sociality, without a determined factor, they are most attempting to participate with genuine personal partiality to that environment. But in cases where one cannot broach an aspect, system, or object in a manner of complete general sociality, one requires a determinant system that follows a succession of sequences that do not default directly into general sociality.

The Role of Future Rewards and Succession

The foremost example of this is the corporate system, which in its proper function gains engagement from direct action of general sociality. The determinant factor is defined as the very instance of dictating the system that does not define itself by general sociality but is determined by its very composition to provide an outcome that is altogether distant from current happiness. It is not the case of a determinant factor being already the supposition of a corporate structure, because it is simply the disavowal of certain parameters for the determinant nature of others, while systems are the attention to a realm that is disengaged from general sociality, not for its determinant nature, but from its internal process of functionality. The determinant factor is defined by what psychologists' reference in terms of future rewards, which in our case is not necessarily the willingness to push off in order to receive greater rewards, but rather to proceed upon a platform that does not connect to a logical reference of current stature. In the case of future rewards, it is true that it is the willingness to forgo a current reward for a greater reward, but in fact, if we follow the function, it is the destabilizing of the entire social reality, such that the intermediate stage between the lower reward and higher award is a lack of logical sequence for their psychology. For what is that state of mind between those two realms other than non-reward direction itself, and therefore it is of general specialty?

The reward function that psychologists are focused upon is the provision of that determinant which, in the usual case, is when one is seeking out a reward, but it is not always the case, for it is simply the determinant factor of a different forum, whether it be reward, non-reward, or indifference to its participation and later psyche succession. One can simply mention the formation of general sociality without reference to how it provides for later provision, because in fact the intermediary stage between the provision and the severance is in itself an ambiguous state of the psyche. This would not be considered for anything of reward or non-reward function. And in total, we do understand this, for most of the time there is a factor in it, not necessarily the experience of a reward provision, but rather the decline and degeneration of the entire system. One is retreating upon general sociality from which they came, and thus is ready for the next moment of succession towards a new formation of the determinant factors.

CORPOREAL AND THE LIMITS OF SOCIAL INTEGRATION

To maintain a corporeal system, mutual modality must take place. If it were to rely on its insular internality, it would degenerate by its lack of social adherence, whether conceptually, like in the case of law, or in actuality, like in the case of a marginalized city or state. Take the duty of a guard at a gate, to be simply acting as though a gate would act, with only the accessibility of those proponents of its internal apparatus allowed entry and those that are not to be barred does no service to its corporeal system. It must have a bearing on the social circumstance, and the only way to do such is through the constituents who blur that line. For the internal members are simply aggrandized versions of its assembly, and those who are not are simply barred entry.

The social integration to a corporeal system is the quintessential focus for the animacy of an entity, and any deviation could prove its degeneration. All the while, such is necessary for the social adaptation of that entity, which may have general sociality or fringe socially depart from that institutional basis to conjecture beyond or without that mode of knowledge. More like in how one may attempt the position of professor, with an adaptation of knowledge that may in fact be important to the student body, for example, an honorary doctorate, but was not initially integrated from the institutional standpoint, such that their conjectures are ad hoc to the entire social system despite sensibility of its logic.

Even those who have been a part of that institutional process, when without complete adaptation of that modality, their later conjectures will not be based on a conformative base of corporeal knowledge and would in fact be troubling to the social system. If one never partook, for instance, in an institutional understanding of the basis of violence in the political apparatus with the complication it involves in the justice system, they may conjecture for other proceedings of violence without that detailed understanding of its inherent basis. That is, it is never upon the individual to proceed with violence, and in the occasion of the political juncture of such, it is powered to be least individualistic as possible; most heavily reliant on the political embeddedness and the imparting of the entire system.

When this is adequately understood, by in fact participating in these institutions, then the procession or ideation of individualistic or non-system-based violence would never be entertained. This does not mean there is no logical procession for political violence at a group or individual level, but that is not a logical sequence based on proceedings through an understanding of the basis of the entire system.

If we were to take this example to its completion, we can say that individualistic or group violence is problematic on a conscious level, for only conceptual violence leads it away from the notion of murder in the sacrificial sense; more so that the notion or requirement of renunciation is already existent and not needed for another occasion of such. We could create a whole dissertation on the reasons that such is inadmissible, but that would discount the premise of this argument, which already was brought about from outside a learned basis of the system to which this logical formation is being applied.

We may need such dissertation in the event of a stranger and their logic being presented to us, to which we must be self-aware in how such was a determinate consequence of the corporeal system. Yet that would simply be an intellectual rebuttal, only to become more self-aware or to be freed from the seeming logic that is being presented. But by no means is this a formidable threat to the system, and the dissertation is simply not in response to that. The recognition that this formation of logic is being presented without adequacy to the system to which it is being presented is enough to prevent it from proposing any harm or disruption; akin to a child questioning why they cannot cross a street. They have not the awareness of cars and infrastructure at the level to which they can make an informed decision; such that the only competent answer to such a child is one of determinate consequence, without a logical attempt at answering the question.

It is not like the parent does not contain the knowledge of such reasons, but more so that the child is not available to all that information; and more so in its integration for real life decisions. It can be that the parent can take the question and embark on a journey of becoming self-aware of the systems they are embedded within, but they do so for intellectual development, not for the sake of the child or in proving their logical formation; since the parent understands the feebleness of a child and would not question or assert their capacity to be something that is integrated into the system to which they are asking the question. Only in the case of pronouncing a logicality that is anchored and based on the system of inquiry does such become an important conjecture of understanding; because they are aligning with the corporeal structure and still have reached some conjectures, akin to the adult who questions the rules of the road. They will, in totality, gain a grasp on the understanding of the street, but may do so because even with all of their embeddedness they seem to think that such rules have gaps within it, such as jaywalking or right-of-way.

To be a part of an institution is not very much as it appears, by being a member, citizen, or other informal or formal entity for integration. We may notice that in proportion, not many citizens of a state are part of that institution as it were to be a corporeal bearing for all their understanding. Alternatively, there are those that are not citizens of a state who may even be located outside its boundaries but because of an integration to its parameters, it becomes possible to be 'institutionalized' without location, membership, or any other indicator of integration.

A corporeal structure is inherently conceptual and its material manifestation are not its consequence but rather its byproduct. Rome in some sense still exists, as does Greece, and for that matter, Egypt, all the while the citizens of Rome, Athens, or Alexandria may have not incorporated themselves into that system; maybe even less than the contemporary individual in their understanding of these corporeal systems. It is true that the Roman citizen will have been usurped into the Roman system such that in all their actions it can be correlated to the Roman system, and this is not true of the contemporary individual. This is not due to an understanding per se, but more so to the influential parameters, such that the citizen still does not enjoy the corporeal aspects of the Roman system, even as they are a part of it.

While the contemporary individual may enjoin those aspects for the benefit of their existence despite the lack of influence. This is the same for a student in a university that does not adhere to its institutional parameters, which will nonetheless be influenced by that university as they are embedded within it. However, they will not enjoin that corporeal structure with little consequence other than the influential parameters. They are 'institutionalized' by influence, which we term as university students, but are not subjectively institutionalized and will not have much of an influence in their later proceedings. We will not be able to view them in later analysis, once they have moved beyond that institution, as post-university students, because they will have little bearing on such proceedings.

Corporal and Sentiment of Social Deviation

In the event of deviation from general sociality, that is, when there is a lack of integration either with its infrastructural setting or with the sentiment of its social conceptualization, then the formalization of consciousness will take an intermission. If it is the cause of a social sentiment such as a holiday, seasonal change, or other sort of high social event, then despite the infrastructural setting available for its determinate sociality, it deviates yet maintains its setting as such with its sentiment being the deviation itself.

A major example of this is war, epidemic, or other catastrophe, which is very much a social sentiment and not so much a structural one, unless war enters into the infrastructural realm and disrupts it, which is known by the ancients to be the culmination of wars: burning down the city. For it is finally at that end that warfare disrupts the structure itself. But till then, it simply remains a social sentiment that is afforded to the interest of the social interaction with the catastrophic or tragic sense; that will be defined by its general sociality.

In the case of infrastructural degeneration, that is, when there is an available general sociality to receive and partake with infrastructure, but is the mishap of infrastructure itself that does not allow for its proper permeation. Most of civilized history, and especially in its marginalized setting, is the case of available general sociality that maintained an infrastructural reciprocity; it has not been acclimated into a corporal or embodied social sentiment.

We may take it for granted that there is a system that is available to provide a corporal structure of general sociality, but it is, as far as history goes, an anomaly and difficult to come by, for it is a complex system that is reliant upon a genuine form of tradition.

The reason that tradition is so paramount for corporal embodiment is despite the fact that it would seem that general sociality would be more important as a traditional value, corporal structures require all the details of sociality in regards to its dynamical inference of the habitat to which they translate from that general sociality. They cannot simply take a single sentiment of general sociality and covert it into a corporal system because that system requires many different reference points from the traditional process that brought about adjacent sentiments towards general sociality.

For example, certain classical texts serve as a corporal reference to one's experience, such that it is in reading it, not for the information but rather in how it references itself throughout one's lifetime in regards to the other times in which it references itself, as well as in what way it matters to their parents and tradition. The term *makeup* of a corporal structure is in itself pieces of sociality that are in relation to the major encapsulation of general sociality as it were in the current moment.

There is not one point in a corporal structure that is not in reference to a purposeful aspect that associates with its relationship toward current general sociality. The structure, as a construct, is in itself not bound to change or alteration because it is more based on psychological and biological circumstance, but in how it manifests in its details: all in relation to general sociality and therefore needs to maintain its traditional value. General sociality does entertain the notion of a tradition, but it is not entertained at the moment based on its tradition, because it is not required, but rather in how it intersects at the immediate moment.

There is difficulty in ascertaining what constitutes a social sentiment that does not have correlation with a corporal embodiment, as where would that social sentiment derive its permeation from, but rather in how it is proceedingly intersected with a corporal construct. General sociality does not arrive without corporal constructs because it requires a basis of information which then becomes incorporated as an internal form that is then recycled as something nuanced and distinctive.

It is the example of university: the first year is simply to acclimate to the corporal setting, rather than do anything else; you're having a second year of generating some social nuance in relation to that institution, but still based on the institutional structure; and then finally the disenfranchisement from that corporeal construct, to which one enters into a state of symbiotic relationship to themselves and the material. This is not correlated in any way to the corporeal information, but in itself does have some sort of lineage back to that corporeal construct. And in effect, the social manifestation of that regard is to be considered the true social sentiment that culminates from the corporeal construct, which is then inserted back into the corporeal system by interacting based on that social sentiment through its construct.

Without the initial exposure of the institution, they would have no availability of generating a social sentiment other than in relation to another construct that was inherently based on a corporeal construct at one point or another.

A child without any institutional training, whether by family or by society, will be able to generate social complexification but is found not to do so because they are not generating a form of relevance in how they embed themselves into the surrounding reality. This is a reality that is not available to interact in any other manner other than through a corporeal construct. One cannot simply enter into reality, as it were, without its corporeal construct, as if it would be possible that one would be born in a desert but then be able to interact with what is considered a desert without any infrastructural or institutional setting to determine that.

The initial corporal structure, let us say of the university, was initially a matter of general sociality, and to be precise, an example based on medical institutions which were based on churches and which were based on forms of religious temples. Even religious temples were based on a sentiment of a public that was then institutionalized based on that sentiment, such that we find that the final university is a corporal structure based on all those social aspects.

However, in each of the cases of social sentiment, it was initially based on the entrenchment of an initial corporal structure that allowed for that determinate value. This is why we are forced to always ascertain that the hero is not better than a sort of complex corporal structure, whether being born in a palace, raised in a palace, participating in the upper strata of social relevance, or any other complex corporal structure, because the hero is considered one who carries probable social sentiment and can only do so based on their initial training within corporal structures. There is no contemporary hero that does not do so, but if we follow the fact that they were raised within the infrastructure of a city, then that would be the complex infrastructure that would be considered enough to culminate in their social sentiment based on the hero status. Or they are the anti-hero, based on the fact that they have difficulty in acclimating to corporal structures yet still have the ability of attempting to do so.

A corporal structure becomes diluted when it lacks the social inference; when general sociality or social sentiment do not entertain an acclimating preference towards its structure. The animation of a corporal structure is in how it references itself to social reference. And we can imagine a corporation, for example, that follows an initial social sentiment but becomes corporal in the sense of following the sequence of that sociality without much reference to a further generation of sociality; such that it becomes repetitive of its corporal themes to a point where it loses all substantiation of sociality.

DISJUNCTION FROM GENERAL SOCIALITY

The benefit of a corporeal construct is that it facilitates a form of sociality that does not partake in general sociality. General sociality is defined by its permeable substantiation that facilitates a very present and ongoing discourse, with its vulnerability being that it retains the present movement and its highlighted variation. In any conversation or social interest, it would not necessarily be the basis of anything more than the peak representation of the full form of sociality, but it is highlighted in that direction, which would be catastrophic for a corporeal process to incorporate, that being the highlighted variation, in contrast to the multitude of layers that purport themselves behind that specific variation of sociality.

We could view this instance in any interest. For example, if sociality is interested in a specific film, it is not the film itself that constitutes general sociality, but only that it reached the peak representation, termed the highlighted variation, which has an overlay with little to do with film or any art form, but rather the wholeness of general sociality. Although those layers are not present in ongoing movement, because they do not move but lie behind the movement itself, they thereby cannot be considered for discourse.

Much like this work itself, which is not presented as a part of social discourse, but rather purports the underlying layers of sociality, so that it cannot be considered a highlighted variation but only a consideration for specific layers of current sociality. Even the concept that we are discussing, of corporeal constructs, will be found in most highlighted variations of current sociality, because we would not explore this research subject if not for our own basis within current sociality. However, being that this is the case, we still do not purport general sociality and its highlighted variation, but only that specific layer which we are attempting to discuss. Thus, this entire thesis is a corporeal construct itself.

For example, a lawyer's office is a corporeal construct which does not follow general sociality, for it may be directed in any which way, one being outside the realm of law, another being in direction of law irrespective of lawful practice. It facilitates, as a corporeal construct, a sociality that follows a sentiment of the general sociality but without the highlighted variation of that sociality.

With the sociality within the office falling into its internal system, it enables a discourse and embodiment of an illustrated general sociality that can follow the nuances. In this way general sociality can continue unabated, and this domain can retain its directed structure. In general sociality, there is surely an overlay of law that participates in its dynamics. For if flow were not present in general sociality then there would be no facilitation to have a corporeal construct which follows a directed sociality; one which does not report any retraction to general sociality. But law is not the general assembly of such sociality; it is only one of many, many overlays.

The law office can now take that specific overlay, purported sociality, internal to its structure, to then give access to its details as though individuals carry the individuality of that sentiment. This is why we find that law practices most attuned to the highlighted variation of general sociality will, in fact, be the most undistinguished law practices. Despite the contrary indication of being practices most aligned with general sociality, because they are most parallel they fail to provide an embodiment of any sociality different from the highlighted variation of general sociality. Moreover, they recalibrate that highlighted variation as if it were internal to their own system, when in fact it is not, and instead move on its own accord, irrespective of any specific corporeal construct.

However, those least aligned with general sociality, (the least connected to a participant in an overlay of the highlighted variation of general sociality) constitute the most rigorous law practices. Yet they may lose substantiation through their unavailability of internal socialization. In a more dramatic sense, they may have no use for civilization, for they do not support a sociality that contributes to civilization.

Although they may be reported as necessary for the function of sociality, for example, tax law, such an overlay in general sociality is not found cumbersome, but rather as a backstop to the function of governance and systematic affairs. The entire aspect contained by general sociality in regards to tax law is in itself an institutionalized construct. Therefore, fairly little makes its way into general sociality because it is already a corporeal construct of itself.

Therefore, it is upon general sociality to make the case for a directed sociality toward overlays such as tax law, because it participates already as a corporeal construct. If we are to then create a corporeal construct in respect to that already formatted construct, there is little more need for embodied sociality, which either was taken care of by general sociality or ignored because of a lack of substantiation of its considerable nature.

This is why bureaucratic institutions under the government institution, which is already a corporeal construct under the governmental corporeal construct, do not have to have much reason for sociality because of their second-degree nature. It is upon the governmental construct itself to facilitate a sociality in regards to its bureaucratic elements, which, internal to the bureaucratic system, has little sociality to perform.

The governmental corporeal construct is then the embodiment of the political institution in respect to general sociality, and general sociality always has an overlay of its political aspect, thus making the governmental institution a quintessential construct. However, the bureaucratic construct, which is but a semblance of the corporeal format within the already existing governmental construct, will have no general sociality to report back upon.

Despite the fact that the bureaucratic institution is the one most integrated with general sociality and its infrastructure setting, does not follow the sociality of that general society but rather follows the overbearing constructs of the political institution. It does not have the ability to socialize anything directly from general sociality. Although, when it does attempt to do so, it loses its internal structure as an institution and instead seeks vitalization from general sociality at the individual level.

This is the dichotomy of bureaucratic institutions, which do not have in themselves a vitalization for sociality and usually will resort to embodying aspects of general sociality; despite the fact that they do not act as institutions directed from general sociality. The same can be said of tax law, which is a secondary corporeal construct because it falls under the already existing corporeal construct of tax itself, which is a governmental institution. Its sociality takes its vitalization from general sociality, not as an exemplification of that sociality or its interests, but rather to disenfranchise the institution itself in order to have certain vitality of any regard. In some sense, we could say general sociality has never been interested in the success of a bureaucratic institution other than in the most admissible way of dealing with the political overhead.

That is the essential point of the matter: where, internal to the corporeal construct, is a sort of individuation; it is as if that overlay in general sociality is now becoming personified between members of the corporeal construct, to the extent that it is now as if it has been activated, despite being separate from and disenfranchised by general sociality.

The individuation of the corporeal construct is going to allow a representation of aspects of general sociality, which in its raw form cannot be represented without including the highlighted variation. General sociality is represented by highlights of variation; so that if a specific interest is directed, or a political notion is foremost, it is that which represents general sociality, and none else.

If that were simply the case with corporeal constructs, this would be the only representation of society, and that is all infrastructure would follow: the highlighted variation. And when that variation changes, all infrastructure would need to recede to allow for the next highlighted variation; which can change moment to moment and is impossible to build stable infrastructure around.

We can even say that this very dichotomy, of having served the corporeal construct a place of infrastructure in its overlays of general sociality is itself what allows civilization to thrive. Without that system in place, we would be bound to the highlighted variation of general sociality, unable to enable constructs, whether socialized or infrastructural, to take the place of the general overlays of that sociality.

Thus, general sociality will degenerate itself by simply highlighting its variation. Once we notice an interest, all other interests subliminal to it will be lost. This is because they are not retained by the sociality: variation was highlighted. Or they were meant to be contained by constructs other than general sociality and there are none.

We can see this clearly in the Islamic Golden Age. Although it inherited the intellectual tradition from the Romans and Greeks and extended it through the medieval period, it did not confine corporeal constructs to embody aspects of sociality. As a result, general sociality and its highlighted variation took center stage, despite the prevalence of academic development. It was not that academic institutions did not exist, but rather that there were not enough corporeal constructs to embody the complexity of general sociality, thereby making it vulnerable to highlighted variation.

All it took was a couple of philosophers to purport a sentiment, which was then entertained as the highlighted variation of general sociality, even against the academic development itself. There were no constructs to embody that development, and so it dissipated without remembrance. All the scientific projects, which, as any scholar would say, were ahead of their time, did not take hold in the infrastructure as constructs. In some sense, there were scholars, but no institutionalized constructs to embody the scholarly work. Therefore, it is almost as if they do not participate in the tradition; from the Greeks and Romans to the Christian Enlightenment.[2]

Yet, the corporeal constructs are not "real" in the sense of following general sociality, but are significant for allowing a social system external to itself to follow an overlay of general sociality; so that general society can move with whomever it chooses to highlight, without the consequence of the general system dissipating.

Although general sociality contains overlays of a law embedded in it, it does not report from that vantage. All law forms that participate in general sociality purport an internal sociality that takes that legal overlay as its aim, according to its pedigree, so that it is enabled within civilized society despite the movements of general sociality.

When general sociality needs to infer from that overlay, it need not look far; and when it needs to move away from it, it is already following its own system, and thus remains largely unbound by those constructs.

To obtain general sociality, all we need to do is remove all corporeal constructs, and thus we will find the process of general sociality; more so, its highlighted variation. Because most of infrastructure is constituted as corporeal constructs, there is a very skeletal structure that can be constituted as general sociality. For if we even enter the domesticated room, we have moved into the domesticated elements of general society.

Because of this admixture, one may presume that when they approach infrastructure, they believe that it purports itself as a singular structure, when

---

[2] al-Ghazali, Abu Hamid Muhammad. 2000. The Incoherence of the Philosophers.

in fact, based on the corporeal structures; it is rather a two-part system. One part is constituted by the internality of the layers of general sociality, and the other is general sociality *as it were*. When we remove domestication itself as simply the diminutive structure of general sociality, we are left with a frame of reference that is almost difficult to accept.

In two ways can this admixture arrive at its degeneration: one is the overbearing presumption that the corporeal constructs *are* infrastructure, to which general sociality need not be mentioned or recognized. Although the overlays are obtained, and highlighted variation may seem like general sociality is functioning, it is merely the highlight of variation of corporeal sentiment, cuckolded into a single encapsulation.

Although we may assume that corporeal constructs cannot have highlighted variation, they cannot purport sentiment onto sociality, it is possible that sociality can accept a corporeal *as if* it were a part of general sociality, but more so as its highlighted variation. And in this way, they have lost all bearing of general sociality. It is fairly difficult to distinguish, unless one maintains a distinctive access to general sociality in contrast to the purported sentiment emanated from corporeal constructs.

Even political interests or sentiment can be elicited from a corporeal construct rather than general sociality, simply because it is thought by a populace as being part of sociality, when in fact it is simply a direction that has been taken by corporeal institutions. While other aspects of political interest will form from general sociality itself and may not be a public interest; because, in fact, the public believes that the corporeal proportion is exemplifying general sociality.

We could follow why the populace is following a corporeal exemplification, which would give us access to general sociality. But as the case was in itself, they are following it because they believe that is the highlighted variation of general sociality. When we study it, we only gain access to it as an existent overlay of a more elaborate theme of general sociality, which the populace has not believed to be such; for they do not understand the difference between corporeal constructs and general sociality.

Let us take an example. For instance, if a leader of a state made a statement, it is not already the case that *that* is the politicized sentiment. Therefore, it is the highlight of variation of general sociality but varies depending on the situation. In some cases, it may be that it is simply the proportion of the governmental construct that is exemplifying its internal waste product upon general sociality. Or it could be the case that it is that very corporeal construct which made itself recognized to general sociality, to a point where this statement exemplifies that sentiment.

A general theme to understand whether a highlight of variation is emanating from general sociality or if the case is based on corporeal constructs is in how the populace responds. A drastic or dramatic response will not be the case for being a highlight of variation, for the populace endures singular embodiments of general sociality. That there is a differentiation would lead up to a highlight of variation of that inclusive setting, to a point where they would find a certain complexity in dealing with the highlight of variation. If they are not finding such complexity, it would usually be the case that they are following a corporeal performance; because that can gain leadership amongst the populace without any differentiation. For in fact, there is no sociality in a body that hierarchizes itself at the level of highlighted variation.

Just to make note of this again: all sentiment that emanates from corporeal constructs will participate in some layer of general sociality, especially if a populace is interested in it. But it is for the populace to decide whether that is a highlighted variation; which needs to be decoupled as a peak representation of general sociality, or simply a performance of an overlay.

For example, if a law firm happens to exemplify some legal aspect that reaches the interests of populists, it could be the case of simply the populists picking that purportment as if it were a highlight of variation; because of sentimentality more so than its actual status as a highlight of variation.

Major shifts in a state, for example, financial crises or war, will always be an exemplification of general sociality and not emanating from corporeal constructs. This is because of the complex intersections that they rely upon. The case cannot be made that such events do not have their place in every aspect of a populace. However, with less intersection and reliance upon specific corporeal constructs, such as specific industries, it can be with some suspicion that the performances are not emanating from general sociality, but rather are part of an overlay that takes place within general sociality.

This would be the complexity of having an admixture of infrastructure integrating both general sociality and corporeal constructs.

CORPOREAL PERSONA AND SOCIAL EXPOSURE

In the usual case, where sociality that is exasperated throughout the perceptual realm is limited, this discussion becomes less significant. However, when sociality is streamlined throughout a structural system, it becomes the natural development that individuals, that is, persons, will inhabit a corporeal persona in the adaptation of selfhood within that environment. To experience individuality as though it were distinct, and availability for the exchange of that sociality, is not a natural inclination. For one, there is no ability to experience distinct individuality in such a locale; and two, the exchange of that sociality is complex and requires a continuous contextual form to regulate its process.

For example, if a young adult, or for that matter any person who is sexually active, finds themselves exposed to pornography, it will be an exposure that would have a decoupling of sense because of the effective nature of that exemplification. It would only be for one who is either sexually inactive, overly exposed, or with a formidable context to approach the subject without it being the cause of exposure. This applies the same to high degrees of sociality, which is the pornography of social experience, in that it would be those with limited social function, the overly exposed, or those with a formidable context who will control that exposure.

For those who are not aligned socially, whether emotionally, biologically, neurologically will not be exposed to such sociality. That is, a general child will not be exposed to sociality in the same capacity, for they are not socially developed. However, in the regular case, where sociality is one's function, the only choice is to contextually regulate that sociality. Overexposure is simply the disruption of one's sanity, just as in the case of overexposure to pornography, which corrupts one's sexual faculty. In the case of continuous exposure to sociality without regulation, one's psychological state will become corrupt.

The other option is for one to construct a corporeal persona, as though they are a standing corporation in that environment, and will lose availability to direct sociality as well, to whatever remaining individuality exists outside of that. Contrasting with the regular corporeal venture, which is objective and stands as though a structural inference, the corporeal persona does so from within the subjectivity of the person. They create a split in their perspective of self and generate a branding for the persona to become separate from the regular rumination of the psyche. They act toward the persona, and the persona regulates the other parts of the psyche. As with any corporeal function, this persona utilizes the sociality from its surrounding environment, but in this case, it is the reception of two forms of sociality: that which is outside the person, and that which is within the person, which is sequestered from normal interaction.